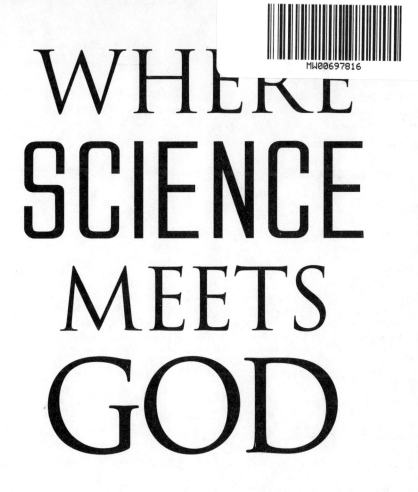

WHERE
SCIENCE
MEETS
GOD

12 WAYS SCIENCE
REINFORCES LDS DOCTRINE

SCOTT R. FRAZER, PhD

CFI
An imprint of Cedar Fort, Inc.
Springville, Utah

ISBN 13: 978-1-4621-2220-2

Published by CFI, an imprint of Cedar Fort, Inc.
2373 W. 700 S., Springville, UT 84663
Distributed by Cedar Fort, Inc., www.cedarfort.com

LIBRARY OF CONGRESS CATALOGING-IN-PUBLICATION DATA

Names: Frazer, Scott R., 1956- author.
Title: Where science meets God/Scott R. Frazer, PhD.
Description: Springville, Utah : CFI, An imprint of Cedar Fort, Inc., [2018]
  | Includes bibliographical references and index.
Identifiers: LCCN 2018010152 (print) | LCCN 2018014352 (ebook) | ISBN
  9781462129249 (epub, pdf, mobi) | ISBN 9781462122202 (perfect bound : alk.
  paper)
Subjects: LCSH: Religion and science.
Classification: LCC BL240.3 (ebook) | LCC BL240.3 .F735 2018 (print) | DDC
  261.5/5--dc23
LC record available at https://lccn.loc.gov/2018010152

Cover design by M. Shaun McMurdie
Cover design © 2018 Cedar Fort, Inc.
Edited by Kathryn Watkins and Allie Bowen
Typeset by Kaitlin Barwick

Printed in the United States of America

10 9 8 7 6 5 4 3 2 1

Printed on acid-free paper

DEDICATION

started writing this book with the idea that only my wife and children might someday read it. Then I came to hope that my grandchildren, as they reached adulthood, might read it too. In the end, I set the goal to write the book to be interesting enough to be read by future generations I will never get the chance to meet. But honestly, if no one else in the world reads this book besides my immediate family, it is still worth my effort. I want my children and their children to find joy, contentment, wonder, and appreciation while on their earthly journey. So I hope these thoughts help my posterity to better understand the universe, the gospel, and how they fit together. Family is everything and I dedicate this book to mine. Thank you, Cheri, Trent, Janae, Morgan, Chris, Sean, Jessie, Michele, and Caleb. I love you all.

CONTENTS

PREFACE

AN INTRODUCTION

As you begin reading this book, you may think it is a book on testimony and faith, simply disguising itself as a book about science. After you have read a few chapters, you may change your mind and decide it is actually a science book disguising itself as a book about religion. I hope that is what you conclude at least. The debate about the alleged conflicts between science and religion has gone on for decades. While there are many books that deal with the overlap of science and Christianity, there are relatively few that address the overlap of science and the gospel of The Church of Jesus Christ of Latter-day Saints (LDS). One of these earlier books, *Can Science Be Faith-Promoting?*, was written in 1935 by Sterling B. Talmage.[1] The conclusion of Talmage's book was that science could indeed increase a person's faith. I hope this book continues the effort to help faithful Christians see that scientific truths will strengthen faith and testimony.

I am a convert to the LDS Church. My decision to convert to the Church was the result of, first, analysis and deliberation. I considered the similarities between the early church that the Savior personally established and the LDS Church today. I studied the need for a restored church and the logic behind that restoration. After that thought process, my second step was to pray about the truth of the Church and the Book of Mormon. In one of those prayers, I received a spiritual confirmation, something for which I will be forever grateful. I discovered then that enough information for the mind and a spiritual witness for the spirit were a powerful combination in convincing somebody of the truth. I have now been a member of the LDS Church for 40 years.

Though I try to be so, I am not a particularly spiritual person. That may be because I am always a scientist and often a cynic. I have my Ph.D. in analytical chemistry and have made a career of collecting data, weighing the evidence, and coming to conclusions about the truth of my little slice of research. With data that I have personally collected, I have constructed multitudes of spreadsheets and plots, all to weigh the evidence until there was enough to form a defensible conclusion. In the realm of science, physical evidence is everything and spiritual feelings do not account for much. Conclusions are not respected unless you have the tangible proof to back them up. In the realm of religion, spiritual evidence is continually sought. But evidence from the sciences should account for something too. We are to be a people who "are truly humble and are seeking diligently to learn wisdom and to find truth" (D&C 97:1–2), for which we will be blessed.

So we must have faith that religion and science are always reconcilable. We have the witness of many Church leaders in regard to such a belief. John A. Widtsoe stated in the preface of one of his books, "This volume is based on the conviction that there is no real difference between science and religion. The great, fundamental laws of the Universe are foundation stones in religion as well as in science."[2] Ezra Taft Benson was equally straightforward in a 1966 General Conference: "There can never be conflict between revealed religion and scientific fact."[3] Spiritual truths cannot conflict with truths uncovered by scientific endeavors.

Therefore, this book is about developing a mental testimony. Many members of the Church "feel in their hearts" that the gospel is true and there are hundreds of books written about developing a strong spiritual testimony. This is a book about "knowing in your head" that God lives. We will consider the evidence of God's existence that has come to us through findings from earth science, biology, ancient texts, geology, food science, and genetics. The goal of this book is not to prove the gospel, but rather to update some of our knowledge about it. This book is about how the findings of science can provide evidence of God, improve our understanding of His ways, and help us to deal with the challenges to our beliefs that are to come. Two scriptures, one a definition and the other a promise, best describe our journey ahead.

> And truth is knowledge of things as they are, and as they were, and as they are to come. (D&C 93:24)

> If thou shalt ask, thou shalt receive revelation upon revelation, knowledge upon knowledge, that thou mayest know the mysteries and peaceable things—that which bringeth joy, that which bringeth life eternal. (D&C 42:61)

NOTES

1. Sterling B. Talmage, *Can Science Be Faith-Promoting?* (Salt Lake City: Free Thinker Press, 2001).
2. John A. Widtsoe, *Joseph Smith as Scientist* (Eborn Books, 1908, 1990), 1.
3. Ezra Taft Benson, *"Conference Report of April, 1966."*

1

A Mental Testimony

cience can teach us a lot of things, but it can't teach us everything. Science cannot answer questions involving ethics or morality, such as what is fair, moral, or the right thing to do. Science cannot point a telescope into the heavens and detect if there is a God there. There is no instrument that can detect a spirit in your body or a meter to verify spiritual power or communication in prayer. Science cannot prove the existence of an afterlife, despite the many books written on hauntings and near-death experiences. On the other hand, scientists have collected more than enough evidence to prove that evolution actually occurred. But proof of evolution is not proof that God does not exist. Numerous scientists have written about the evidence of evolution and then expressed their own testimonies (either pro or con) about the existence of God. But in reading such books, we have to differentiate between statements that are data-based proofs and others that are simply opinions.

Our scriptures and religion teach us a lot too, but they do not teach us everything either. The scriptures do not tell us how the universe was formed or how life came to be on the earth. Religion cannot reveal if evolution occurred, how Adam and Eve came to be on the earth, or if pre-Adamites were here before they arrived. We do not know how Adam's progeny actually spread across the planet or the size of the flood that Noah survived. We do not even know the history of the books of the Bible for many hundreds of years after they were written. Many of the disputes between science and religion arose because each side claims to have answers that they cannot support. Admittedly, this book is yet another review of the overlap between science and religion. But hopefully you will find that this book explains how the two can mesh together to find resolution instead of dispute.

No one can prove conclusively that God exists, of course. God has purposefully established our mortal life so we cannot have a provable knowledge of His existence. But He has invited us to look for evidence of Him and He has even told us where to look (Moses 6:63). When you follow His clues, you still can't prove His existence beyond a reasonable doubt. But the only alternative theory to God's existence is that the universe, the earth, life, and mankind exist as a result of random, undirected events. The odds of that theory *can* be proven to be very low and the findings of several sciences will be used to establish that proof. Though few are aware of the change, research is providing us data that can be used to support God's existence. This book is dedicated to helping faithful Christians to interpret and deal with findings of sciences that often challenge some very personal interpretations of the scriptures and how we live. We must always remember that the goal of any science is to uncover truth. Why should a non-scientist Christian care about science? Because testimonies can be fragile and one should strengthen theirs whenever possible. Science can help in that effort.

This book is built on the premise that every Christian actually has two separate and distinct testimonies. Generally, when we discuss testimonies, we only think of our spiritual testimonies. These testimonies are developed and grown by receiving inspiration from the Holy Ghost. These are the verifications from God that what we are learning in any given Church meeting, scripture study, or prayer is true. We cherish these spiritual witnesses that we have in our lives and, with each and every prayer, seek for additional spiritual strength.

Besides having a spiritual testimony, recognizing and seeking to grow a mental testimony is important as well. To use the "heart and head" metaphor, when you have a spiritual testimony, you have faith in your heart that the gospel is true. When you have a mental testimony, you are convinced in your *mind* that the gospel is true. Your heart will seek for spiritual witnesses to continue strong in your faith. Your mind, on the other hand, will demand information, evidence, and logic to continue to be strong in your conclusions. Science can strengthen your mental testimony by providing such information. Your approach to science will determine if it is helpful or not to your mental testimony.

Rarely do we differentiate the two testimonies in our Church meetings or scripture study. But as we read the testimonies in our scriptures and other Church books, we can see that some are mental testimonies and some are spiritual. As an example, Joseph Smith had a very strong mental testimony. In Joseph Smith History 1:25, he very clearly bears this mental testimony,

> I had actually seen a light, and in the midst of that light I saw two Personages, and they did in reality speak to me . . . I have actually seen a vision . . . Why does the world think to make me deny what I have actually seen? For I had seen a vision; I knew it, and I knew that God knew it, and I could not deny it, neither dared I do it. (Joseph Smith—History 1:25)

This was not a spiritual revelation given to Joseph; he doesn't even mention the Holy Ghost in this account. He saw a light and then two Personages with his eyes. He heard Their words with his ears. That experience was forever lodged in his brain and could not be denied. So, through his trials, when Joseph's spiritual self was weakened and he began to question his calling, he could lean on his strong mental testimony for support. He had seen what he had seen. Actually, miracles of any kind would contribute to a strong mental testimony. After witnessing the events on the Mount of Transfiguration with the Savior, we can be sure that Peter, James, and John had very strong mental testimonies. They had witnessed the Savior shine like the sun and had seen Moses and Elijah. A voice from the heavens had declared to them that Jesus Christ was the son of God (Matthew 17:2–5). It would be difficult to deny such an experience.

But, let's face it, miracles like these are rare. What have you actually seen with your eyes or heard with your ears that you could include in a description of your own testimony? We believe in the Church that members should always strive to strengthen their spiritual testimonies. Though they would be really amazing to see, we cannot wait for miracles to occur to bolster our mental testimonies. But there is other evidence that our minds can consider. So, if the mind demands information and evidence to be convinced of a truth, how do we strengthen a mental testimony? Where do we look for this evidence?

As mentioned, in the last century the findings of science have been used by critics to attack the religious beliefs of faithful Christians. In past decades, these attacks have crushed the mental testimonies of many Church members, who then reconsidered, and often abandoned, their spiritual testimonies. These sad stories have led many faithful Christians to either simply refuse to listen to what science discovers or to attack every new discovery with uncompromising, fundamentalist denial. These people have stopped trying to build their mental testimonies so that their spiritual testimonies could remain isolated and unaffected. It is a disturbing approach that does not encourage our learning process, which we should actually be striving to improve. I have even heard Church members criticize the value of mental testimonies, declaring that testimonies should be based only on the witnesses of the Spirit and not conclusions of the intellect. But testimonies are very personal and individual. For me, my mental testimony is as important to me as my spiritual testimony. If my beliefs cannot stand up under the test of time and the discoveries of new truths, then my beliefs need to change. These changes are *not* rationalizations, designed to allow you to cast aside religious commitments as outdated and old-fashioned. These changes should be viewed as a reconciliation of new truths and old perceptions. Truths that appeared to be in conflict are brought back in harmony with one another.

There are two requirements to strengthen a mental testimony. First, you must be willing to collect information and insights that describe truths within your physical world. As you see alignment of the findings of science with what you know from scriptures and revelation, your mental testimony will increase. It is like putting together a puzzle. The pieces from your spiritual life of Church meetings and gospel study start to fit with what you are learning from academic study. At first, not all of the pieces will be a perfect fit. Some of these new truths will not at first synchronize into your present perceptions of this world, how we got here, and what we should believe now that we're here. When that happens, you need the flexibility to adjust your conclusions, no matter how long you have held them close. The perceptions you will be asked to change are not basic principles of the gospel.

As an example, in 1530 Nicolas Copernicus collected his astronomical observations and concluded that the earth revolved around the sun. This conclusion contradicted the teachings of the Catholic Church. Church authorities pointed to the scriptures that supported the idea that the sun circles an immovable earth.

> One generation passeth away, and another generation cometh: but the earth abideth forever.
> The sun also ariseth, and the sun goeth down, and hasteth to his place where he arose. (Ecclesiastes 1:4–5)

> Say among the heathen that the Lord reigneth: the world also shall be established that it shall not be moved. (Psalms 96:10)

So, Christians of the time had to make a choice. Were these scriptures actually establishing the design of the solar system or were they simply making the point that the Lord reigns over the earth forever? As more astronomical information verified the earth indeed orbited the sun, Christians adjusted their interpretation of these verses. In doing so, our understanding of the universe and its mechanisms became more accurate. We need to go through this same process today. Science reveals new observations about our mortal existence and we reevaluate our understandings (and the scriptures that back them) to reconcile whatever differences exist. Yet, change is hard and this is not an easy process. But with each adjustment, our mental testimonies get stronger and tougher to shake, because they are based on truth.

To start this testimony-strengthening process, we will review some of the scientific findings of the last couple of centuries that have challenged scriptural interpretations and religious beliefs. We will review how the inevitable scientific/religion conflicts formed and how they have been resolved (by many faithful Christians at least). One can find a similar pattern in how this resolution occurs. First, you should confirm what science has actually revealed. Science usually takes years to work out the difficulties in new theories. Sometimes we have to be patient for this to occur. Secondly, you have to compare the new discoveries to your religious beliefs. Do they really disagree?

While we may be more willing to change our personal interpretations of the gospel, most Church members are much more protective of their Church doctrine. But what is Church doctrine? In his book *Determining Doctrine*, Dennis B. Horne lists hundreds of quotes by Church authorities over the years, discussing that very question. My favorite quote is the following from Robert L. Millet.

> In determining whether something is a part of the doctrine of the Church, we might ask, is it found within the four standard works? Within official declarations or proclamations? Is it discussed in general conference or other official gatherings by general Church leaders today? Is it found in the general handbooks or approved curriculum of the Church today? If it meets at least one of these criteria, we can feel secure and appropriate about teaching it.[1]

Did you notice the use of the word "today" twice in this quote? With that definition in mind, we have to continually reassess our understanding of Church doctrine. Is it Church doctrine that the earth was created in six 24-hour periods? Is it doctrine that Adam started out as a clay statue before he became a man? Is it a doctrine of the Church that Noah's flood covered the earth from the North to the South Poles? Sometimes it is hard to separate truth from tradition. For example, the scriptures make it pretty clear that the wise men were not present at the birth of the Savior, though almost every Nativity scene in the world contests that fact.

With that goal in mind, in the following chapters I will try to present a fair consensus of the findings of several sciences. We can then examine any reconciliation of those new findings and old perceptions. Oftentimes that means going back to the scriptures and asking yourself, "In light of this new information, how will my interpretation of these scriptures change?" Having done this a few times, I give examples of my own thought process while doing such a review. You can hopefully use this discussion to establish your own foundation on which to build a stronger mental testimony.

There is a final reason to learn how to resolve conflicts between science and religion. In regard to scientific findings and a changing world, the hardest is yet to come. The sciences, especially biology and genetics, will mount serious challenges to many of our religion-based understandings of life. Geneticists are developing the technologies to create plant, animal, and human life in test tubes. In 1997, a ewe named Dolly was cloned at the Roslin Institute in Midlothian, Scotland. This event raised many questions regarding whether men should play God and tamper with the process of creating life. Is it morally right to clone human beings? Or is it acceptable in the eyes of God for us to tamper with DNA and change the blueprint of a human infant? Research has continued to develop the abilities to carry out such tasks, but it has been seriously hampered by preventative legislation. Governments cannot answer these moral questions, so they have passed laws to prevent cloning, stem cell research, and other DNA-manipulation until someone else can figure out the ethics of such work. But the inevitable day will come when someone crosses those lines despite the laws. Learning how to build and sustain a religious mental testimony around what science has provided us so far will be good practice in dealing with the future.

It is difficult to consider new ideas and concepts. It is difficult to tackle difficult ethical questions and moral dilemmas that face us today. But, I think it is our responsibility to do so—as human beings, as parents, and as believers in God. When children and friends come to us with questions about life, God, and the universe, it is sad to admit that we "haven't thought about it much." We need to learn about the issues, think about them, and resolve them in our minds as best we can. Omar Bradley, a general in World War II and the first chairman of the US Joint Chiefs of Staff, illustrated this point in 1948. He refers to the creation of the nuclear bomb, which had just been used to end the war with Japan. But his words could be applied to any of the scientific breakthroughs we are about to discuss.

> Our knowledge of science has clearly outstripped our capacity to control it. We have many men of science, but too few men of God. We have grasped the mystery of the atom and rejected the Sermon on the Mount. Man is stumbling blindly through a spiritual darkness while toying with the precarious secrets of life and death. The world has achieved brilliance without wisdom, power without conscience. Ours is a world of nuclear giants and ethical infants.[2]

The world around us is becoming more complicated each day. We can hide from the changes, but they will find many of us anyway. You may have a nineteen-year-old daughter who is taking a biology class at an out-of-state college and is questioning what she learned in Sunday school about the beginnings of life. You may have a friend at work who loves history and asks how you can believe in scriptures that are not supported by historical facts found in other ancient manuscripts. Your spouse may be receiving radiation treatments for cancer and your doctor has suggested stem-cell treatments. Your mother may have had a stroke and is being kept alive by life-support. What do you do? It is a different world and old perspectives that have served us well in the past are not going to answer these new questions and challenges. In the following pages, we will consider an approach to develop new and more durable perspectives about how religion and science interact in our lives.

ALMA AND KORIHOR

In the Book of Mormon, Alma chapter 30, we find an interesting argument between the prophet Alma and an atheistic church critic named Korihor. Korihor accuses Alma and other church leaders of promoting the worship of God and the Savior just to make money from their false teachings. In verses 37–38, Alma verifies that Korihor is indeed an atheist. In verse 40, Alma then asks him for some hard evidence to support his atheism.

> And now what evidence have ye that there is no God, or that Christ cometh not? I say unto you that ye have none, save it be your word only. (Alma 30:40)

Well this is an interesting turn of events. Normally it is the atheists who demand proof of God's existence from the religious faithful, not the other way around. Korihor has no proof that there is no God, so in verse 43, Korihor tries to turn the tables on Alma and demands that he provide evidence of his own.

> And now Korihor said unto Alma: If thou wilt show me a sign, that I may be convinced that there is a God, yea, show unto me that he hath power, and then will I be convinced of the truth of thy words. (Alma 30:43)

So, both Alma and Korihor are asking each other for evidence of their beliefs. Alma then responds to Korihor's challenge, with a scripture that will set the tone for much of this book.

> But Alma said unto him: Thou hast had signs enough; will ye tempt your God? Will ye say, Show unto me a sign, when ye have the testimony of all these thy brethren, and also all the holy prophets? The scriptures are laid before thee, yea, and all things denote there is a God; yea, even the earth and all things that are upon the face of it, yea, and its motion, yea, and also all the planets which move in their regular form do witness that there is a Supreme Creator. (Alma 30:44)

So Alma presents four pieces of evidence to Korihor as proof of God's existence:

1. the testimonies of his brethren and past prophets
2. the scriptures
3. the earth and all things upon it
4. the planets of the solar system

We learn a few lessons from this story. First, Alma reveals that, if we are looking for evidence of God's existence, we first have *spiritual evidence* from testimonies and scriptures. Secondly, we have *physical evidence* that can be found on the earth and in the heavens. Thus, we need to consider both types of evidence and remember to respond to Alma's challenge to investigate, "the earth and all things that are upon the face of it, yea, and its motion, yea, and also all the planets . . . ."

To continue the story, Korihor sadly did not accept the evidence presented by Alma and again demanded a sign. Those familiar with this narrative know that this demand for evidence did not work out well for Korihor. The sign he received was that he became deaf and dumb. With that curse, Korihor was cast out, became a beggar, and eventually met a tragic death.

Granted, Korihor was not a man on a sincere mission to seek for God. But what was Korihor's sin? What did he do to deserve his fate? Yes, he demanded evidence of God's presence—but many people are seeking evidence of the truth of God's existence. In fact, we are taught to do so. The difference was that Korihor demanded that his proof be immediate and on his terms—and that is not how one collects evidence of the existence of God. It takes time, study, contemplation, and prayer to figure these things out. The irony behind this story, as pointed out by the chief judge in Alma 30:51, was that though Korihor's sign was immediate as he requested, it was certainly not on his terms. If you are not willing to be patient in collecting both spiritual and physical evidence of God's existence, then you will almost certainly fail.

So I would like to follow Alma's counsel to search for evidence, first in others' testimonies and secondly within the heavens and earth. Before doing so, it is necessary to better define the weighty principles we are discussing and consider why God doesn't just give us all the answers.

A WORLD OF FAITH— THE NEED FOR DOUBT

The word "doubt" is normally used to mean a deficiency of faith and is almost always cast as a weakness that we should avoid. Nephi reproves his brothers for doubting their mission to retrieve the brass plates (1 Nephi 4:3). The Savior chides Peter for his doubt as he was sinking beneath the waves of the stormy Sea of Galilee (Matthew 14:31) and Thomas for his doubt after the Resurrection (John 20:29). The two thousand stripling warriors were successful in battle because their mothers had taught them *not* to doubt (Alma 56:47). There seems no doubt about it—doubt is bad.

But doubt is, in fact, an important part of the equation of life and learning. Alma tries to explain the relationship of faith, doubt, and knowledge in Alma 32. First, Alma defines faith as a belief in things that are not seen but are true.

> And now as I said concerning faith—faith is not to have a perfect knowledge of things; therefore if ye have faith ye hope for things which are not seen, which are true. (Alma 32:21)

Then Alma explains why the world needs to be a place of faith and not of knowledge.

> And now, how much more cursed is he that knoweth the will of God and doeth it not, than he that only believeth, or only hath cause to believe, and falleth into transgression? (Alma 32:19)

There has to be doubt in the world, because if it was a place of perfect knowledge, all men would be cursed for their disobedience. Faith gives men who do not want to follow God a chance to change their minds at a later time. Faith gives men more time to learn wisdom and, with that learning, conclude that they should choose righteousness. If a man has no faith, then he can shy away from the things of God until he matures enough to realize what he is missing. If a man has much faith, it gives him time to grow closer to God, without having to yet live at the level of commitment a perfect knowledge would require.

But faith is to be strengthened so it can approach the goal of becoming knowledge. Alma uses the example of nourishing a seed. As we accept and live the gospel, we learn that each principle (or each seed) gives our lives meaning and joy.

> And now, behold, is your knowledge perfect? Yea, your knowledge is perfect in that thing, and your faith is dormant; and this because you know, for ye know that the word hath swelled your souls, and ye also know that it hath sprouted up, that your understanding doth begin to be enlightened, and your mind doth begin to expand. (Alma 32:34)

To rephrase, faith is what we have *before* we have a perfect knowledge. Faith needs to be gradually "grown up to be a perfect knowledge." When our faith grows up to become knowledge, our faith becomes dormant. We don't need it anymore.

To follow the process, first God wants us to *want* his promises to be true. We call that "hope." In gospel-based discussions, we hope for future events. We hope that the Second Coming, Resurrection, and exaltation will come. But, since all these events are in the future, hope still includes doubt. But our hope leads to faith—a belief that the scriptures are true, that our prophets are prophetic, and that we have the gospel plan that will lead us, through obedience and prayer, to the celestial kingdom. Faith describes our belief in past and present events. We believe what our scriptures and our Church leaders tell us is true. Again, there is still a lot of doubt mixed in with faith. But there is a good reason the Lord included so much doubt in our mortal probation.

If we are motivated by hope and faith to seek knowledge, then it will come. When we have overcome the hurdle of doubt that God has placed in our path, we shall have our reward. Doubt has done its job and will gradually, but gracefully, bow out of the picture as we gather knowledge.

A business analogy may explain this principle. Let's say that you are interviewing for a new job with a start-up company. The president of the company describes the job to you. The responsibilities are significant, but you can handle them with diligent attention and hard work on your part. The pay is fair and almost everyone in the company seems friendly. Little deliberation is necessary to decide that you want to take this job. Then the president explains one final detail—due to financial constraints, all your pay will come at the very end of your first year. Though you realize that sacrifice and loans from your parents may be required, you still think it worth the extra effort.

But there is doubt that the company will be viable enough for you to be paid at all. Is it worth the risk to work for a year with the possibility you won't be paid? What do you do? Well, you probably talk to others who know something about the company. You study the history of the start-up, trying to determine if it is based on good business principles. You try to determine if the company is worth the risk of a year of your devotion and hard work. The doubt drives you to work more diligently to learn about the company, its president, its beliefs, and its practices. With some trepidation, you take the job and start working. As you work at the job (but still continue your research), you gradually realize the company is sound. Not only is it sound, the company is ethical, your coworkers are great, and you are a better person for working there. Your pay hasn't changed and it is still possible that you won't ever see it. But you feel pretty sure that will receive your reward. It is worth the risk. Doubt has driven you to the extra effort of study and work and you are a more dedicated worker because of it. First, you had hope that it was true, which led you to have faith that it was true, and then, in the end, you will have a knowledge that it was true.

In a world without doubt, everyone would be taught from childhood that there is an absolute certainty that God lives and that heaven has been proven to exist. If you lead a good life, without a doubt you will obtain your reward. From that fact, most men and women would then conclude that a life of righteousness is a very logical strategy. People would attend church regularly, avoid alcohol, live a moral life, and obey the commandments, because they would know with absolute certainty that there is a heavenly prize for their righteousness. Tithing would be considered a good investment, since everyone would know that there will be a good return on their money in the next life. Obedience would be based on the logical conclusion that there will be an eternal reward to make that righteousness well worth the trouble. People would be living the gospel for all the wrong reasons.

God wants us to follow Him and obey the commandments, but He wants us to do it for the right reasons. Our Heavenly Father wants us to be righteous not only for the heavenly reward, but because we love Him and really want to become more spiritual beings. He wants us to continuously seek communication with Him. He wants us to seek after a more spiritual life, filled with prayer, study, service, and compassion. He wants us to love our fellow man and to leave behind our ambitions, love of material possessions, and pride. He wants us to live our lives such that the celestial kingdom is a continuation of the life we lived on the earth and not just a prize for following the rules. If being righteous and attaining the celestial kingdom was only the result of a risk/reward analysis, there would be no need to seek out a spiritual life.

God did tell us that heaven awaits the obedient. Indeed, attaining the celestial kingdom is an important motivator for the faithful to follow the commandments. But God introduced enough doubt into the earthly plan for us to continually question if God exists, to wonder if there is a life after death, and to have to search for defensible reasons to continually obey His commandments. He introduced enough doubt about His existence and a gospel plan that any logical person who does not seek after the spiritual evidence available to him will probably decide that God does not exist. We are required to first have faith, and not a perfect knowledge, as we navigate through earth life.

So we live in a world of faith, where doubt must exist. We cannot prove the existence of God because the world was *purposefully set up that way.* Thus, you will not see spirits or resurrected angels walking the streets of your community. You will not see heaven-sent miracles on a daily basis and any miracles you do witness will almost certainly have natural explanations for them. Subsequently, anyone who wants to find the truth of God's presence must seek evidence of truth, strive to understand it, and confirm it in their meditation and prayers. In the end, we must each come to our own conclusion, which is exactly what our Heavenly Father wants us to do.

At no time in earth's history could mankind be allowed to "prove" the existence of God, as such proof would end the probationary aspect of this life. A vital part of the plan was that God did not want man to be able to know without a diligent search that He lives and that a celestial kingdom awaits those who are faithful. In that life-long search, we gradually remove doubt from our hearts and minds.

To conclude, there is one more scriptural reference we can make to explain the relationship between faith, doubt, and knowledge. In the book of Ether we learn of the brother of Jared, "a man highly favored of the Lord" (Ether 1:34). This man attained a level of knowledge that allowed him power to see through the veil which separates this world from the spiritual world.

> And because of the knowledge of this man he could not be kept from beholding within the veil; and he saw the finger of Jesus, which, when he saw, he fell with fear; for he knew that it was the finger of the Lord; and he had faith no longer, for he knew, nothing doubting. (Ether 3:19)

The brother of Jared had accumulated knowledge "and he had faith no longer, nothing doubting." Knowledge removes doubt, it provides understanding. Knowledge replaces faith and it gives power. It is a life-long pursuit, but well worth the effort.

REMOVING DOUBT—THE NEED FOR EVIDENCE

The Roman goddess Justitia, or Lady Justice, is depicted as a woman with a scale in one hand and a sword in the other. The scale is used to measure the strength of evidence of one argument against the evidence of another. The side with the strongest evidence, and thus the better and weightier argument, should always win the debate. Most depictions of Lady Justice have her blindfolded, signifying that guilt and a just punishment should be determined impartially. In any debate or trial, only the evidence should be weighed.

But courtroom dramas that we see on television are only suspenseful because good evidence is hard to define. For example, it is the prosecuting attorney's job to argue that the accused is guilty, just as it is the defense attorney's job to argue otherwise. Obviously, they are both extremely biased in their opinions. So, even when these attorneys give their testimonies in their summaries at the end of the trial, a wise jury will know that those opinions are not good evidence of the guilt or innocence of the accused.

Impartial witnesses to a crime are certainly less likely to give a biased opinion than attorneys are, so their testimonies can be given more credence as good, admissible evidence. But even witnesses can get it wrong. Are they biased for or against the accused in any way? Do they have a grudge against the accused? Do they remember events correctly? Then you also have physical evidence, which can be most convincing. If there is video of the accused man pocketing the allegedly stolen item from a store or if the accused was found with the stolen item is his possession, it is much easier for the jury to reach a verdict. Physical evidence itself is unbiased. But physical evidence is also mute; it cannot tell you from where it came and it can be misinterpreted.

Evidence is important when it comes to religious discussion as well. On one side of the debate on religion, we have millions of Christians who have had spiritual experiences that were very meaningful and real to them—and they are more than happy to bear witness and testify of their beliefs. This I will call spiritual evidence, which generally comes from your own feelings of the Holy Ghost or from listening to others' such experiences. On the other side of the debate we have millions of skeptics. They will not accept the testimonies of others as proof or evidence of God's existence. They want physical, tangible proof of His existence. But the skeptics are not necessarily correct in their skepticism. There are times, as described by Alma, you can obtain evidence from the testimonies of your brethren.

EVIDENCE IN OTHERS' TESTIMONIES

Returning to the story of Alma vs. Korihor, Alma asks his opponent why he wanted a sign "when ye have the testimony of all these thy brethren, and also all the holy prophets?" Obviously Korihor was a skeptic and the testimonies of others did not convince him. But in our own search for truth, should others' testimonies qualify as evidence? Can the opinion of other people, be they friends or strangers, strengthen your *mental* testimony? The rest of this book is about the evidence of God found in the sciences. But a few words should be said about the difference between mental and spiritual testimonies. Your mental testimony is more . . . skeptical than your spiritual testimony. The logical mind wants to hear some proof behind what is being taught.

For example, like many members of the LDS Church, I think it is cute when little children get up to bear their testimonies. Sometimes you get to hear some interesting insights from little children. In those moments, I may even feel the Spirit witnessing to the innocent sincerity of that child or the simple truths of which they testify. But I do not believe that my *mental* testimony is strengthened by hearing the witness of a young child. A naturally skeptical mind is not cruel or uncaring, but it does realize that this child has a more limited knowledge and understanding of the world than most adults. Much of a person's testimony draws from their life experiences, and most children are still developing their testimonies in simple matters that were relevant to me when I was their age. Similarly, in a college course, we would insist on being taught by a professor who has studied the subject for many years rather than a child who has only had basic lessons on the subject in elementary school. Our logical minds expect our teachers to be knowledgeable and experienced. Their teachings and witnesses will mean more to our mental testimonies than those of a child.

Let me tell you about the man whose testimony I personally value above all others. President Henry B. Eyring, presently a member of the First Presidency of The Church of Jesus Christ of Latter-day Saints, is named for his father, Dr. Henry Eyring. President Eyring often recognizes his father in his talks for being a good father and role model. Dr.

Eyring, who passed away in 1981, was a renowned chemist as well. He was a professor at Princeton University for 15 years and then became the dean of graduate school for the University of Utah. In the course of his career, Dr. Eyring did ground-breaking research in his chosen specialty of physical chemistry. The goal of physical chemistry is to determine the laws, physics, and principles that govern how the atoms and molecules of matter interact and why chemical reactions occur. Physical chemists achieve this by formulating very complicated mathematical equations that describe the movement and reactivity of atoms and molecules. These equations describe the molecular interactions that are required for life to occur. Dr. Eyring was one of the best in his profession. If you read any physical chemistry text, you will surely read about the "Eyring equation," which describes in mathematical terms the relationship between reaction rates and temperature at the molecular level.

Dr. Eyring, a man who understood the laws that hold the universe together, was also a very active member of the Church. He wrote about his beliefs and testimony in his book *Reflections of a Scientist*.[3] As a fellow scientist, my respect and admiration for Dr. Eyring makes his testimony very meaningful for me.

When I hear someone bear their testimony, I am in the same position as a jury trying to decide if a witness is credible. We may realize the witness is sincere in his beliefs, but we don't know if those beliefs are good evidence of truth. Perhaps an example is in order. If I was to tell you, "I have a real million-dollar bill in my wallet!" would you believe me? My declaration *is* a pretty incredible claim. Is my witness good enough for you? Do you believe my testimony? A quick inquiry with your smartphone then verifies that there is no such thing as a million-dollar bill. I somewhat grudgingly admit to you that, no, I don't have a million-dollar bill in my wallet. "But," I exclaim, "I do have a $10,000 bill in my pocket!" Do you believe me this time? Is my witness still acceptable? Probably not. Your opinion that my testimony is good evidence of truth has taken a serious blow. The value of my declaration to your mental testimony has diminished due your recent experience with me. Thus, though my testimony is always important to *me* as evidence that God lives, my witness may or may not be acceptable as evidence *to you* of God's existence.

In summary, yes, testimonies borne in Church meetings, one-on-one talks, Church videos, or in books can be considered good evidence that God lives and the gospel is true. It can be helpful to seek out those people you hold in high regard, for their teachings will be especially meaningful in realizing that the gospel plan is real. But how much truth you will assign to other people's words depends on who you are and how you think. Just how skeptical are you? For the most skeptical of us, others' testimonies will not be enough to develop a conviction of something as important as whether God exists or not. In the viewpoint of a true skeptic, a person who witnesses of God's existence can be brainwashed, carried away by emotions, ignorant of scientific findings, or simply misled by religious fanatics and zealots. So, for these people at least, the testimonies of other people are not enough. Thus we need to look for other forms of evidence.

EVIDENCE IN THE EARTH

As we have already discussed, this earth had to be a world of faith and, thus, doubt. It could not be obvious from living on the planet and simply looking around that God had created the earth. Thus, God had to carefully "hide His tracks." He had to create the world but leave little evidence of His involvement. To do this, God used purely natural means to organize this planet and the life upon it. All evidence suggests that God used natural laws of physics, chemistry, and biology to create this beautiful world. Each process was a wonderful tool. The laws of astronomy and gravity placed the planet Earth in its correct place in the solar system. Biology, genetics, and evolution placed life on the earth and sifted through that life to select species that were best adapted for their environment. Each science was used so that mankind could uncover and explain each step in the Creation process.

Mankind, as he developed his sciences, has been able to look very carefully at every bit of evidence of how the world was created. We have examined our own world through geology, radiochemistry, paleontology, and genetics to name a few. We have studied other galaxies to get hints of how ours developed. Scientists have discovered and unlocked the mechanisms of almost every natural process found on earth. Have we found enough evidence to prove conclusively that God exists? No. Does this surprise anyone? It shouldn't.

Yes, God covered His tracks well. But He has left clues within the earth and heavens that bear record of Him—and He has invited us to find those clues.

> And behold, all things have their likeness, and all things are created and made to bear record of me, both things which are temporal, and things which are spiritual; things which are in the heavens above, and things which are on the earth, and things which are in the earth, and things which are under the earth, both above and beneath: all things bear record of me. (Moses 6:63)

The Lord uses the word "things" *nine* times in this one sentence, which is a word used when one simply can't be any more specific. Those things would include other planets and galaxies that are above the earth, plants and animals that are on the earth, and fossils that are under the earth. All those things, when their complete stories have been uncovered, bear record of God. They are a proof of His existence and His accomplishments in creating the earth. But we have to be willing to learn those stories. How can we learn of "things which are in the heavens above," but through reading an astronomy book? How can we learn of "things which are on the earth," without some understanding of biology? From where did the plants and animals originate and how do they witness of God? Finally, how do we understand the meaning of "things which are under the earth" that bear record of God without knowing the findings of geology and fossil discoveries, which teach us about the history of the earth and the processes of developing life?

There is another reason to be aware of the findings of science. Over the last century, many people have taken the findings of science to prove their contention that God does *not* exist. The books and press coverage regarding these conclusions have resulted in severe cases of cognitive dissonance in many faithful Christians. Cognitive dissonance is the mental conflict caused by trying to hold two opposing beliefs in your mind at the same time. It is a frustrating situation and your brain will make every effort to resolve the discomfort. If your religion is teaching you one thing and science appears to be teaching you the opposite, cognitive dissonance is bound to occur. Unchallenged, such dissonance has shaken the mental testimonies and then spiritual testimonies of many faithful Christians. But that is only because these people have accepted conclusions based on faulty assumptions and limited data. Thus, if we want to be prepared, we must strengthen our mental understanding of God's creation process such that we can proficiently respond to challenges of God's existence. Science is not an enemy of religion. If we look at the more recent findings of science in the studies of our world and universe, we will find that it can actually contribute to a deep conviction and mental testimony that God created it all.

So, first we have to believe that there are many things in the world—and above it and under it—that bear record of God, as mentioned in Moses 6:63. Secondly, we need to understand that God *wants* us to learn of those things.

> And as all have not faith, seek ye diligently and teach one another words of wisdom; yea, seek ye out of the best books words of wisdom; seek learning, even by study and also by faith. (D&C 88:118)

There are numerous scriptures like this one that encourage us to seek wisdom and learning out of the best books. The Lord did not say to seek for only religion-based wisdom or learning. The implication is that any wisdom or learning will increase our faith and knowledge. Truth is truth and all truth bears record of God. God wants us to gather knowledge and wisdom so that we are prepared to endure, and even respond to, the arguments of men.

> I tell you these things because of your prayers; wherefore, treasure up wisdom in your bosoms, lest the wickedness of men reveal these things unto you by their wickedness, in a manner which shall speak in your ears with a voice louder than that which shall shake the earth; but if ye are prepared ye shall not fear. (D&C 38:30)

If you don't have knowledge and wisdom prepared, then wicked men can tell you things that can shake you to your core. But if you are already aware of the issues that these men may reveal, you will have a reasoned response for them. Their questions need not be bothersome nor unsettling. The things we learn in Church meetings, scripture study, and prayer can be combined with what is learned from science to gain stronger mental and spiritual testimonies. When we take the Lord at His word that "all things bear record of me" and we study those things, we can come to realize how well the pieces of spiritual learnings fit together with those from science to give us a more complete perspective of this life, the earth, and the universe.

EVIDENCE IN SCIENCE

The way the generously-used word "science" is used in the media, we may think that Science is a well-managed organization based in Washington DC. But science is actually a loose consortium of workers pursuing knowledge by research, experimentation, and study in many diverse areas. It includes research and development in medicine, chemistry, electronics, nutrition, astronomy, and engineering. Industry and commercial interests, such as pharmaceutical companies, pursue science to develop products and make a profit in selling them. Other scientific knowledge, mostly gathered in universities and other academic institutions, is gathered simply to advance our understanding of history, religion, society, and human behavior.

The general public and science have had a turbulent relationship over the past several decades. The public loved science and technology when man first landed on the moon in 1969. As a nation, we were proud when *Columbia*, the first space shuttle, was launched in 1981. But we were horrified when the space shuttle *Challenger* exploded early in its flight in 1986, dealing NASA a public relations blow from which it has never recovered. We have cheered the medical sciences as they developed treatments for cancer, AIDS, and diabetes. Despite its complexity, we now take organ transplant for granted, which has saved the lives of otherwise terminal patients. There are few people in our country who have not benefitted from the medical advances of the past 50 years.

Unfortunately, many topics of scientific study have become issues of political debate. When the findings of science do not agree with the desires of a large segment of the public, then science becomes the target of scorn and ridicule. But while the whims of the public and the resulting political climate can change at any time, truth cannot. Despite the pressures, science cannot change the results of its experiments, nor should it try. Truth is truth. At various points in history, the general public has been told that science is represented by evil business interests whose mission is to pollute the environment, take advantage of the less-educated, and mislead the public.

So, to establish a few facts as a foundation of our discussions, I would like to present the following statements—all of which have all been disputed by numerous critics at some point in our history (and even today).

1. The earth is round, not flat.
2. The earth rotates around the sun.
3. Smoking causes lung cancer.
4. Men did land on the moon in 1969.
5. The vaccine for mumps, measles, and rubella does not cause autism in children.
6. Genetically Modified (GMO) food has not harmed anyone and is safe to eat.
7. Global warming is real. The burning of fossil fuels has increased the level of carbon dioxide in the atmosphere which has led to verified increases in global temperatures.

Most of the world has finally accepted statements #1, #2, #3 and #4. Incredibly, statements #5, #6, and #7 are still under debate in many political circles and internet blogging sites. But there is more than enough data to establish the truth of these statements. Global warming is probably the most recent, still-debated issue. Following the same pattern of past attacks on scientists who declared unpopular truths, climatologists have been accused of creating the myth of global warming with the hope of forwarding the agenda of liberals and environmentalists. Since solutions to global warming would be burdensome to our economy and way of life, climatologists have become the scapegoat of many politicians' attempts to simply deny the problem exists. How can climatologists know for sure that global warming is real? Because they have compiled and studied *thousands of pages* of data which follow carbon dioxide levels and global temperatures over the last 59 years. Results are not debatable any longer. Just as we now scoff at the idea the earth was once considered to be flat, future generations will wonder how the people in 2018 could ever be so misled about global warming.

The point is that science has no agenda. Certainly mistakes are made, but scientists monitor each other. If a paper is published that introduces new conclusions and breakthroughs, other scientists will try to reproduce the study. If they are unsuccessful, they will publish their own results and call into question the original study. Others will then follow with their own attempts at the experiment and their own publications. So eventually the truth is uncovered and then reported to the world.

A Challenge to Your Beliefs

For many readers, the study of the sciences may mean a radical change to beliefs that you have cherished for decades. But the change in beliefs, be it by you or your future generations, will be made eventually. Despite the misconceptions and denial of many of the general public, there are a number of scientific discoveries that are theories no more. Over many years, so much data has been collected that support the truth of these hypotheses that there is no longer any credible doubt that they are true. For example, gravity is not a theory; it is a law. If you doubt it, feel free to run your own experiments. The Big Bang, which explains the creation of the universe, is now considered by astronomers to be undebatable in its premise. The basic tenets of evolution, as proposed by Charles Darwin, are not debated in scientific circles anymore. Learning involves a certain amount of change to one's way of thinking. If you try to bend confirmed findings of science to fit your own perceptions, knowledge will move on without you. These next chapters will try to explain to the reader how to make adjustments.

In my discussions with members of the Church over the years, many have a general reluctance to discuss the learnings of science, especially in a church setting. There seems to be a feeling that the two don't belong together. Many members seem to feel that discussing *how* God uses natural means to accomplish His purposes is somehow disloyal to Him. As members who worship their God, it seems we want to believe in the sheer wonder of His power. Many seem to want to believe that God, and even our prophets, will often choose to wield raw power in accomplishing a task. For example, there are still faithful Christians who want to believe that God created the world and everything in it in just six days. What an amazing display of power that would have been! To admit that God actually took millions of years to accomplish this feat through natural means makes some feel that they are somehow diminishing God. It rather depends on your perception of God. Is He a power-wielding being who creates worlds in a few days, or is He a patient God who used natural processes to create worlds for His spirit children?

In every aspect of our lives and in everything we believe, there will be a place where science meets religion. In each chapter of this book we will discuss some of those interfaces—our understanding of the Creation and how we came to be, how we view our scriptures, our diets, and even how we die. Taking them in chronological order, it makes sense to start with a discussion of the Creation. This is a two-hundred-year-old debate, so you may have already read much of the following discussion. But the Evolution vs. Genesis debate is a good example of how science affects our interpretations of the scriptures and understanding of God. For example, unlike a few generations ago, there are only a few people who still believe in a six-day (i.e., 144-hour) Creation. Science has gathered so much evidence to the contrary that only a few remain who argue against the finding that the Creation took much more time than a week. To understand how we got to this point, we need to look back on some of the history of the evolution vs. religion debate. We need this review to understand how science, by continually providing evidence of its claims, changed the thinking of millions of faithful Christians. This process of learning will continue and we need to understand how to reconcile what science can prove as true with what we know spiritually to be true. Then can we apply the scientific knowledge of today to strengthen our own mental testimonies of God. The Creation debate is a good place to start the discussion.

NOTES

1. Dennis B. Horne, *Determining Doctrine* (Roy, UT: Eborn Books, 2005), 126. Original source: Robert L. Millet, "What is our Doctrine?" *The Religious Educator*, Volume 4 #3 (2003), 19.
2. *The Collected Writings of General Omar N. Bradley*, volume 1, 1977 (US Government Printing Office), 584–589.
3. Henry B. Eyring, *Reflections of a Scientist*, (Salt Lake City: Deseret Book, 1983).

2

THE ADVENT OF THE
EVOLUTION DEBATE

For about 6,000 years, men and women looked at the beauty of the earth and the wonders of the heavens and appreciated the fact that God must have made it all possible. The earth and heavens were so grand and beyond the capability of men, that in simply looking at it, one's testimony of God grew. Crops grew from seeds, yet no one really knew how. Flocks and herds of farm animals multiplied. With the birth of every child, parents could see the hand of God. All realized that, though a man and a woman may create life and deliver a baby, they had no idea of how it came to be. Since Genesis had declared that this was all part of God's plan and a result of His efforts, it was easy to attribute the beauty of nature and life to God's grace and care.

Over the centuries, mankind has increased our knowledge and learning about the earth and life. As scientists came to understand the chemistry of how plants grow and the biology of how animals and humankind multiplied, the wonder of the process started to dim. Astronomers figured out the physics of suns and planets and why they moved in the heavens. Biologists were able to explain why seeds sprouted and babies are conceived. Men and women started to lose appreciation for the power behind the creation of the earth and everything on it. After all, once explained, a magic trick is no longer magic. We began to question the need for a God at all.

But insightful men and women realized that, though they may understand *how* something is accomplished, they still needed to explain *who* or *what* directed the effort. Good things rarely happen by chance. Most things in life, left to their own devices, become more chaotic and less organized. There was simply no good explanation of how the earth and earth life could have occurred without a Creator. So during these years of learning, God was still recognized by most as the power and the directing force behind the Creation. For the few atheists of the time, the existence of the universe and earth was clearly the weakest link in their argument that God did not exist. If God did not exist, the faithful asked, then how did we get here? From where did the earth come, with its vegetation and animal life? Then, in the late 1800s, two discoveries brought about new answers to those questions.

EVOLUTION

The idea of evolution did not begin with Charles Darwin. The concept of evolution had been discussed for years; in fact, Charles Darwin's grandfather was a proponent of a similar theory. Farmers of the day already knew that through selective breeding they could develop better-yielding plants and animals. But Charles Darwin and Alfred Russell Wallace were the first men to make the observations and connections that made evolution into the science it has become.

Charles Darwin was born in England in 1809. He graduated from Cambridge in 1831 with plans to become a clergyman. But that same year, Darwin's interest in geology and natural history won him an appointment as the naturalist on the surveying ship H.M.S. Beagle, bound for South America. During stops made in the Galapagos Islands, Darwin observed that each island had its own variation of species of tortoises and birds. As an example, Darwin noted that birds had different beaks best suited to consume the seeds and other foods available on that particular island. This observation is what started Darwin on the development of his theory of the "transmutation" of species—the idea that species could change so much through selection that they could become another species.

Darwin delayed publishing his results for years, understanding that this theory would generate both attention and hostility. Finally, in November 1859, Darwin published his theory in his now-famous book *On the Origin of Species by Means of Natural Selection.*[1] His first edition sold out immediately and evolution starting making headlines. Exactly as Darwin had feared, members of the social elite, scientists, and celebrities worldwide hailed the book as the discovery of a lifetime and removed the need for God in the creation of our world.

The headlines touting evolution over God continued. In 1925, the state of Tennessee prosecuted a teacher named John Scopes for teaching evolution in high school. The trial, commonly referred to as the Scopes Monkey Trial, captured national attention and was seen as a contest between the faithful followers of God and disbelieving evolutionists. In 1960, a movie named "Inherit the Wind," which was based upon the trial, was released. In that movie, the Genesis account of the Creation is mocked and those who believe in it are depicted as seriously unenlightened. The link between evolution and atheism grew stronger.

Over the years, through the continually-growing fossil record, evolution became more and more accepted as a real science. The story was a simple and logical story in progressive development. Single-celled bacteria had become multi-celled organisms and those organisms became small fish and other aquatic creatures. At some point in history, the fish that normally spent their lives near the shorelines ventured out onto land and evolved into amphibians, then reptiles, and then mammals. Finally, in its culminating event, primates, the smartest of all animals, evolved into humans. As would be expected, the fossils of the earlier species were found in the oldest geological layers of earth or sea bottom. The fossils of more evolved species were found in layers formed in later time periods.

Meanwhile, work in another unrelated science made its own breakthrough. In 1953, James Watson and Francis Crick determined that DNA was constructed as a double helix. This enabled scientists to develop better working theories on how DNA was constructed from parental DNA and then passed on to children. In their studies, these early geneticists came to realize that errors could occur in this transcription that let to genetic changes in the progeny. Some of these genetic flaws were fatal. Many produced disabilities in the offspring that prevented reproduction of its own. Still, DNA was seen as the internal mechanism that allowed species to develop new genetic strengths and pass those advantages on to future generations.

However, without a Creator or a Director of this event, it was understood that evolution by genetic change could only be a random, stumbling process. As stated, most mutations would be seriously detrimental to that generation of the organism, causing sterility or death. Very few mutations would be expected to be advantageous to the species and provide them traits that would give them some distinct advantages in survival and reproduction. Then enough of these advantageous changes had to accumulate for the organism to become a new species, separate and distinct from its ancestry. But each and every step of this process had to be a random event. *Wow,* one might think, *the evolutionary path from bacteria to man is a long one and each step was a random, lucky draw of a DNA sequence? Such evolution must have taken a very, very long time!,* thus setting the stage for the next discovery.

THE AGE OF THE EARTH

The third major discovery to fuel the evolution debate was that the earth was much older than had been previously believed. Based on an interpretation of the Bible by Archbishop James Ussher in 1654 and the writings of other biblical chronologists, for centuries we had believed that the earth was created in 4000 BC. This changed in the late 1800s. In 1862, the physicist Lord Kelvin published his calculations that set the age of earth at between 20 million and 400 million years. There was a good deal of debate about the subject, but by 1900 geologists had reached a general consensus that the age of the earth was around 100 million years old.[2] Through the 1900s, the science of radiometric dating significantly and quickly increased the estimated age of the earth. By 1920, the accepted age of the earth had jumped to two billion years. Three elements found in the earth's crust decay slowly but at a very constant rate to become more stable elements: uranium-238 becomes lead-206, potassium-40 becomes argon-40, and strontium-87 breaks down to rubidium-87. By analyzing the ratio of the original element to its final breakdown product, one can determine the age of any given rock. In 1927, Arthur Holmes published a book estimating the earth to be between 1.6 to 3.0 billion years old. In 1956, Clair Cameron Patterson, using uranium-lead isotope dating, concluded the earth was 4.55 billion years old, which is very close to today's accepted age.[3]

These new estimates of the age of the earth arrived as if on cue for evolutionary theory. The two discoveries fit together nicely. Randomly-based evolution must have taken a lot of time, but certainly 100 million years would have been enough time, wouldn't it? New estimates just kept increasing the age of the earth up to the present 4.5 billion year mark, and the case for a creation directed by random evolution got stronger and stronger. Surely, 4.5 *billion* years would be enough time to create all the plant, animal, and human life found at the dawn of history!

THE BIG BANG THEORY

In 1929, a development came from the science of astronomy that broadened the arguments even further. Edwin Hubble (for whom the Hubble Telescope is named) concluded from his observations that galaxies are all moving away from each other. By observing the direction and speed of their flights, Hubble and his associates were able to rewind backward in time to the point where all these galaxies had started their 14 billion-year journeys. To have scattered all the matter in the universe from one point in space to its far corners would have required a gigantic expenditure of power. But from where did all that matter come in the first place? We know from Einstein's $E=mc^2$ equation that a little matter can be created from a lot of energy. With calculations beyond the scope of this book, it was postulated that the same explosion of energy that sent galaxies hurtling into space had also created that matter. These elements, mostly helium and hydrogen, established the building blocks of our universe. In 1949, Fred Hoyle named this massive explosion the "Big Bang," which he meant to be more as a derisive term than an accurate description. But the name stuck. "The Big Bang Theory" is now a well-recognized term, so much so that in 2007 it also became the title of a popular TV comedy.

In any case, with the Big Bang model, atheists of the day now had an explanation for the creation of the universe, our sun, and earth. Their contention was that the Big Bang replaced God as the creator of the universe, just like evolution had replaced God as the creator of earth life. As some saw it, God had become even more unnecessary.

The evolution debates continue even today. As evolutionists tried to take their theories into the schools to be taught to future generations, there was an emotional backlash from the religious community. These debates ended up in the courts and in very loud and uncomfortable public school board meetings. Such arguments made great headlines and the confrontations were well-reported to the world. If evolution had been just another scientific discovery, no controversy might exist. It would be taught in schools with no concerns. But from its beginning, evolution was tagged as the proof that God does not exist and it became a rallying point for atheism. As such, it has received the wrath and indignation of Christians everywhere. Evolution became the sworn enemy of the faithful, who taught their children to stay away from it at all costs. Thus, many faithful believers in God have come to the point of not differentiating between atheists and evolutionists. That is a shame. Because though all atheists may be evolutionists, not all evolutionists are atheists.

BELIEVING IN BOTH
GOD AND EVOLUTION

Today evolution is still depicted as evil by many faithful Christians. There are many, oft-repeated stories about good and faithful youth who went off to college, fell in with a group of radicals, and accepted the doctrine of evolution, thereby losing their faith and leaving the Church. I realize there are many examples of such sad abandonments of God and church. Evolution has been successfully used as a tool to pull people away from their faith. The faulty premise of this choice is that you only have two choices. Either you believe in the Genesis account of the Creation in six days or you accept the evidence-based explanation of evolution. No middle ground was thought to exist.

But many good and faithful Christians, especially those in medicine and the other sciences, have rejected that premise and publicly questioned why they couldn't believe in *both* evolution and God. Couldn't the Big Bang and astronomical physics be the tool that God used to create the universe and our solar system? Couldn't evolution have been the tool that God used to create life on our planet? For years, the two sides of the battle simply ignored such suggestions. The belief on the creationist side was that you either believed Genesis as it was written or you weren't a good Christian. The evolutionists proclaimed that if you believed in the outdated God of the Old Testament, you were hopelessly deluded. The battle lines were drawn and compromise was not endorsed by either side.

The battle lines are still there, manned by Christian fundamentalists on one side and pure evolutionists on the other. However, many believing Christians learned of the on-going discoveries of more fossil evidence and of the observations in astronomy that supported the Big Bang. Their spiritual belief in God was strong, yet the evidence of creation by natural means had become overwhelming. For these people, there simply *had* to be a middle ground. The belief that the universe and earth life were created by astronomical and evolutionary sciences under the direction of God's power has grown in many communities and continues to grow today. The data that has been amassed in the last several decades supports this third option. If science can show the need of a Creator, then science can promote faith. Essentially, the Big Bang and evolution are superb tools that were used by God, the Creator, to accomplish the creation of the universe and a life-filled earth. These tools are the "how" of the Creation; God is the "who."

If a man builds a house, who should get the credit for the building—the man or his tools? After all, unless the man can cut construction lumber with his teeth and pound nails with his skull, his tools are absolutely essential for the work. The man had to use tools and construction materials to translate the house design he had in his head to the actual house itself. Now, if I examine the house, I can tell you what tools were used. By looking at the cuts in the lumber, I can tell you if the man used a radial saw, a hand saw, or an axe. By looking at the impressions of the hammer around the nails, I can tell you if he used a framing hammer, a finishing hammer, a sledgehammer, or a nail gun. Tools leave evidence. But by looking at the house, I can tell you very little about the man who wielded the tools. I can tell you if I like his taste in houses and if he attends to the small details of building a home. But that is about all. The Designer does not leave evidence of His work.

Please note that this viewpoint of God-using-evolution is a win-win proposition. It allows one to have a belief in our Heavenly Father and still accept all of the evidence for the Big Bang and evolution, recognizing them as the tools He used to accomplish creation. So, what has occurred in the past couple of decades to support this God-using-evolution theory?

SIMPLICITY VERSUS COMPLEXITY

William Paley was a very foresightful man whose writings actually influenced Charles Darwin. In 1802, he wrote a book entitled *Natural Theology, or Evidences of the Existence and Attributes of the Deity Collected from The Appearance of Nature.*[4] In it, he put forth what has become a rather famous metaphor. He proposed that if he chanced upon a stone during a walk in the wilderness, he might conclude that it had lain there forever. It was simply a rock. However, if he were to find a watch on such a path, he would have to conclude the watch had a maker. The watch was too complex to have occurred randomly. Nature, Paley concluded, is like the watch—so complex that it had to have a Maker. In 1986, Richard Dawkins, the preeminent atheist spokesman, wrote the book, *The Blind Watchmaker: Why the Evidence of Evolution Reveals a Universe without Design,*[5] criticizing the 184-year-old metaphor. But the metaphor is still applicable today and the question remains. Could a complex universe have been created by random events?

Randomness can only explain simple events. For example, you could flip a coin five times and get five heads. Random chance allows that. The explanation is that you got lucky and random chance allowed you to flip five heads out of five flips. But if you were to flip 10 heads in a row (with odds of 1/1,024) you should probably become very suspicious of the coin. If you were to flip 20 heads in a row (with odds of 1/1,048,576) you would know something is amiss. Statistically there is a one-in-a-million chance that you could flip 20 heads in a row. Admittedly, as they tell you in the lottery ads, it could happen. But it is much more likely that the answer is more complex than simple random luck. Someone has rigged your game. The coin is weighted or the person flipping it is cheating. Speaking of the lottery, statistically it is possible for you to win the grand jackpot. Win it twice and you will certainly be investigated. Win it three times and you will almost certainly be jailed. As a society we believe in the possibility that unlikely events can occur, like winning the grand lottery. We also believe in the impossibility of very, very unlikely events, like winning that lottery twice.

However, through the mid-1900s, no one really believed that the universe, earth, or life was that complex. The universe was seen as a few planets and multitude of stars spread throughout a great deal of space. Since we weren't aware of the complexity behind the universe and its origin, space seemed pretty simple. Earth was certainly a beautiful planet, teeming with life. But it was greatly underappreciated. No one recognized the unique ability of this planet to support life. Many thought that Mars and even Venus could be populated. Life itself was seen as simple. A bacterium was considered to be a cell membrane surrounding a very small amount of salt water and a nucleus, whose functions were only vaguely understood. A plant grew and made chlorophyll. Mammals, including humans, ate, breathed and eliminated waste. The complexity of cell biology, whether of a bacterium, plant, or mammal, had yet to be realized.

So what has changed over the last two decades? Our understanding of the *complexity* of these events has grown immensely. After examining the Big Bang for over 85 years, we have come to realize that it had to be meticulously programmed. Too little force and the expanding universe would have eventually stopped expanding and then collapsed upon itself under the weight of gravity. Too much force and galaxies would never have formed. The strength of gravity had to be exact so that suns could form and the earth would hold us on the ground without shattering our spines. The elements in the periodic table had to have certain exacting properties so they could form in the middle of suns and then provide the building blocks of planets and human bodies.

It has been found that single-celled algae and bacteria are more amazing than we once thought possible. Thousands of biochemical reactions are occurring every second in these cells to collect nutrients, dispose of waste, reproduce, and live their lives. The cells of our body have to do all that and communicate with other cells as well to function as organs and muscles. The complexity of your body is only exceeded by that of your brain. The molecular biology of your DNA is mind-numbing. Your cells have different proteins which mark key locations of your DNA, build it, cut it, and transport it.

The debate between pure evolutionists and pure creationists soon became a question of whether undirected evolution could navigate the complexity of creating the earth, life, and mankind. Besides the watch and watchmaker metaphor, others have been suggested. Could a roomful of monkeys with typewriters write a Shakespearian novel if given a million years to do so? Could a pile of airliner parts hit by a tornado ever end up as a completed Boeing 247 ready for flight? Many such metaphors were followed up by examples of impressive biological complexity, like the flagellum of a bacterium or the mammalian eye. The response to this challenge by evolutionists was to point out that every complex operation or creation can be broken down to a list of simpler operations. This is true. But in the last few decades, those lists have gotten very long. Any model that requires randomness to accomplish such long lists of tasks has lost credibility.

To respond to these poor odds, many atheists, including Richard Dawkins, started talking about parallel universes. Their theory is that of potentially millions of universes that have formed, only a very few universes like our own had all the right settings to support life. This sounds a little like the science fiction books that I so love to read. A much easier and likely explanation was that there was an intelligent, driving force behind it all. However, the word "God" was apparently very hard for some people to actually say. So names like "Universal Life Force" and "Prime Mover" were often used instead. But, under whatever name you choose, that Creator was, of course, God. If you take God out of these equations you are left with randomness as being the driving force behind them. Life and our universe are the most complex things in, well, the universe. Randomness can explain simple things, but cannot adequately account for anything so complex.

Those of us who believe in God and that He used natural forces and evolution to create our earth are called "theists." A Gallup poll of 2014 reported that 31% of Americans believe in theistic evolution. About 19%

did not believe in God or that He was involved in the Creation (atheistic evolution), while 42% of Americans believed God created man as he is, with no help from evolution.[6] Theists who believe in the God-using-Evolution model can range widely in their beliefs as to how much of the Creation was due to God and how much was due to evolution. If you attribute the creation of our earth and life simply to the application of God's power over the course of six days, you ignore all of the evidence that the sciences have accumulated over the last two centuries in support of evolution. If you attribute the creation of our planet strictly to evolution, you remove the need for God (and claim we beat one-in-a-trillion odds to be here). There is a gradient in between those two extremes. God could have been involved every day over the millions of years of the Creation or He could have checked on progress every few million years and made adjustments. Most theists' beliefs lie somewhere on that gradient. But the point is—if you put together all the knowledge that we have today, having God using evolution to accomplish His plan and design is a very defensible position.

THE EVOLUTION OF DOGS

Science has found that evolution is a very powerful tool. The development of the domestic dog breeds in the last few hundred years is a good illustration of that power. Evolution has significantly increased the diversity of dog breeds in a relatively short amount of time. Dogs are, of course, descendants of the wolf. It is believed that several thousand years ago the least human-averse wolves of nearby packs started hanging out around human settlements, eating the leftovers of their meals. Over time, some of these wolves became domesticated and worked for their human masters at hunting, herding, guarding, pulling sleds, and providing companionship. Eventually, it occurred to some of these men that breeding their best herding dogs together gave them even better herding dogs. Breeding their best hunters would result in better hunters and breeding their littlest and cutest dogs would produce even littler and cuter lapdogs.

Some breeds such as the mastiffs in Italy, the Pekingese in China, and the Lhasa apso in Tibet can trace their origins to 2,000 years ago. But most of the present-day dog breeds were started in the 1800s. From an evolutionary standpoint, either 200 or 2,000 years is a very short time indeed to witness the diversity of dog breeds that all started with the wolf. In the course of those few years, the original wolf evolved to become dogs that range in size from the Great Dane to the teacup poodle or the from the thin greyhound bred for speed to the lumbering mastiff bred for war.[7]

But the dog breed diversity illustration is an even better proof for theists than it is for pure evolutionists since dog breed evolution is *directed* evolution. Neither random selection nor the dogs themselves had anything to do with the results we see today. The breadth of dog breeds is a good indicator of what evolution can do. But it is even better proof of the power and ability of directed evolution to arrive at a certain goal.

NOTES

1. Charles Darwin, *On the Origin of Species by Means of Natural Selection* (1859).

2. Brent Dalrymple, *Ancient Earth, Ancient Skies*, (Stanford: Stanford University Press, 1994), 41.

3. Ibid., 164–168.

4. William Paley, *Natural Theology, or Evidences of the Existence and Attributes of the Deity Collected* from *The Appearance of Nature*.

5. Richard Dawkins, *The Blind Watchmaker: Why the Evidence of Evolution Reveals a Universe without Design* Penguin Science, 1986).

6. Frank Newport, "In U.S., 42% Believe Creationist View of Human Origins," Gallup, June 2, 2014, http://www.gallup.com/poll/170822 /believe-creationist-view-human-origins.aspx.

7. Jake Page, *Dogs: A Natural History* (New York: HarperCollins, 2007).

3

A BRIEF NOTE TO CREATIONISTS

Creationism is defined in Dictionary.com as "the doctrine that matter and all things were created, substantially as they now exist, by an omnipotent Creator, and not gradually evolved or developed" and "the doctrine that the true story of the creation of the universe is as it is recounted in the Bible, especially in the first chapter of Genesis."[1] There are many members in the LDS Church who, by this definition, would define themselves as creationists.

The first chapter of the book of Genesis is a literary piece of art. The words in Genesis flow off the page in their description of the Creation. Quoting just the first three verses . . .

> In the beginning, God created the heaven and the earth.
>
> And the earth was without form, and void; and darkness was upon the face of the deep. And the Spirit of God moved upon the face of the waters.
>
> And God said, Let there be light: and there was light. (Genesis 1:1–3)

It reads like a beautiful poem. That's because it *is* a beautiful poem, which is where we need to start our discussion.

MOSES

We believe that Moses wrote the book of Genesis. To do so, he must have been recounting a revelation that God gave him of the Creation. Can you imagine the difficulty Moses would have had in putting into words a vision of that magnitude? Moses would have seen creations involving astronomy, geology, botany, animal biology, and perhaps microbiology that would have required doctorates in all these fields to possibly begin to understand them. Prophets have frequently despaired and struggled at putting into words what they have seen in revelation. For example, Lehi struggled to understand and teach the concepts of his dream. To understand it better, his son Nephi prayed for his own vision and was taught some of the symbolism that Lehi missed (1 Nephi 12:16–18). We can be assured that the apostle John did his best in writing the Book of Revelation. But John had to record a complex, apocalyptic vision with more imagery and symbolism than any other account in the scriptures. He too must have struggled to put that revelation into words.

Moses did not consider himself an eloquent man; he considered himself "slow of speech, and of a slow tongue" (Exodus 4:10). Apparently, he was also a man of few words. Though thousands of books have been written about it, the first chapter of Genesis only contains 797 words. But, as it turns out, Moses was also a poet. Those 797 words are beautiful. Moses's writing was designed to communicate the beauty and majesty of the Creation—and he accomplished that. Moses did not try to explain the details of the Creation. He did not try to nail down the time line associated with the Creation. If you think about it, such detailed explanations would have taken away from the poetry and majesty of his words. If Moses had written a purely scientific or historical textbook, then Genesis would not be the Genesis that speaks to the more spiritual side of our being.

WHAT DID MOSES MEAN
BY THE WORD "DAY"?

I doubt that Moses ever expected that each and every word in Genesis 1 would be examined in detail and hotly debated for thousands of years after his death. But nothing has been debated more than the words, "And the evening and the morning were the first day" (Genesis 1:5). Moses then uses the exact same wording for the other days as well.

Much of the debate between creationists, evolutionists, and those of us in between rides upon the interpretation of this phrase. What did Moses mean? Fundamental creationists interpret this phrase literally—that it means God completed each of His tasks within a 24-hour period. Other creationists take Psalms 90:4 ("For a thousand years in thy sight are but as yesterday when it is past . . .") and 2 Peter 3:8 ("But, beloved, be not ignorant of this one thing, that one day is with the Lord as a thousand years, and a thousand years as one day.") at their word and believe that each "day" was actually 1,000 years.

Many biblical scholars believe that this whole Creation time line debate is based upon a simple mistranslation of the original text. Moses did not write the Bible in English; he wrote it in Hebrew. The Hebrew word "yom" is the word that was translated as "day" throughout Genesis. Translations are rarely simply a word-for-word replacement. Different words may impart different meanings to different cultures. Thus there has been much debate of whether or not the translation of this most important word was accurate. As explained by Francis Collins,

> The Hebrew word used in Genesis 1 for day (yom) can be used both to describe a twenty-four-hour day and to describe a more symbolic representation. There are multiple places in the Bible where yom is utilized in a nonliteral context, such as "the day of the Lord"—just as we might say "in my grandfather's day," without implying that Grandpa lived only twenty-four hours. [2]

The reader should know that this understanding has been around for a long time. In 1967, Dr. Henry Eyring fully recognized this differentiation.

> In the King James version of the Bible, the phrase "creative periods" is rendered as "days." The use of this term has led to at least three interpretations." (First—usual day of 24 hours, second—thousand year periods, third—times of unspecified length) "In earlier times, some variation of the first two interpretations was all but universally held by the Christian world. This is no longer true. In school and secular publications, the third interpretation is the generally accepted one. [3]

In 1908, over 100 years ago, John A. Widtsoe stated, "The best opinion of today, and it is well-nigh universal, is that the Mosaic record refers to indefinite periods of time corresponding to the great division of historical geology."[4] While there may be a handful of fundamentalist creationists that refuse to believe it, it is very widely accepted today that the word "day" in Genesis simply refers to a long period of time.

This recognition does not take the wonder out of the Creation, but it does make it more natural. With so much more time than six days, God did not need to snap his fingers and create a world filled with life. A slower process now opens up the possibility for the Creation to have been accomplished by evolution.

THE BOOK OF ABRAHAM

The book of Abraham offers some interesting insight into the definitions of what night and day may mean in Genesis. Of course, Abraham 4–5 is very similar to Genesis 1–2, but we believe that the account in Abraham retained some concepts that were removed or lost from Genesis. In chapter 4, we find that Abraham tried to communicate to the reader that God was redefining the words "night" and "day"—and they were not the same as our normal definitions. In Abraham 4:5, we read,

> And the Gods called the light Day, and the darkness they called Night. And it came to pass that from the evening until morning they called night; and from the morning until the evening they called day; and this was the first, or the beginning, of that which they called day and night.

Verse 8 gives very similar wording, ending with the words, "and this was the second time that they called night and day." In verses 13, 19, 23, and 31, this same wording is used to indicate the third, fourth, fifth, and sixth time that what the Gods called a night and a day had passed. This wording makes all these verses rather long and tedious. So Abraham must have really wanted to communicate an important concept to have included such repetitive wording six times in this revelation of the Creation. With careful reading of these two chapters, "that which they called day and night" seems to be an intentionally vague length of time. Given that Abraham was seeing a revelatory vision that encompassed billions of years, he probably had no way of measuring the time of any given event anyway. His approach seemed to be to simply explain that time passed during the Creation, the Gods kept track of how long each event took, and they *called* each time period a day and night. Thus the account in Abraham helps us understand that the Gods called the time it took to accomplish a task a "night and day" and each was not necessarily a 24-hour period. Given these additional insights, Latter-day Saints should be comfortable that the word "day" in Genesis should not be translated as a 24-hour period.

After this discussion, members of the LDS faith might be interested in the fact that Joseph Smith first published the book of Abraham in 1842, two years before his death. Charles Darwin published The Origin of Species in 1859, which catalyzed the debate that six days was not nearly enough time for the Creation. As John A. Widtsoe observed in "Joseph Smith as Scientist."

> Now, then, we must remember that Joseph Smith made this translation long before the theologians of the world had consented to admit that the Mosaic days meant long periods of time; and long before geology had established beyond question that immense time periods had been consumed in the preparation of the earth for man.[5]

WOULD GOD HAVE WANTED TO CREATE THE EARTH IN SEVEN DAYS?

If I were God and had a flower seed, there are two ways that I could make that seed become a flower. I could plant the seed and then use my priesthood power to command the seed to grow immediately. If I have the power to do such a thing, within a few minutes that flower would grow and blossom before my eyes. A second approach would be to plant the seed, water it, and simply wait for a few months. The power is already within the seed to grow to be a flower. I just have to wait for it to accomplish the task on its own.

In my study of the scriptures, I don't see where God the Father or Jesus Christ use their powers without cause. When they want something done, they usually call a prophet or other servant to accomplish the task. God does not simply command that men (or the world) immediately become what He wants them to be. I have never read in the scriptures where either Heavenly Father or the Savior were in such a hurry to get something done that they used an outpouring of priesthood power to get it done quickly.

As an example, when the Savior arrived at Bethany to raise Lazarus from the dead He asked in John 11:34, "Where have ye laid him?" Why would the Son of God need to ask such a question? Could He not have paused, consulted the Spirit, and obtained the answer for Himself? But such a display of power and spiritually-attained knowledge was unnecessary. All He had to do was ask the townspeople of Bethany where the body of Lazarus had been placed.

As stated earlier, evolution was the means that God used to place plant and animal life in every corner of the earth—from the highest mountains to the deepest depths of the sea. Evolution is a great tool and appears to be like the seed just mentioned. It just had to be planted and allowed time to grow and carry out its programming. Granted, it would take millions of years to accomplish its task. But is God on a tight schedule? God, who, according to Moses 6:67, is "without beginning of days or end of years, from all eternity to all eternity"? God, who according to Doctrine and Covenants 76:4, "From eternity to eternity he is the same, and his years never fail"?

It is easier for me to accept that God knew the plan and knew that His schedule for the creation of the earth would take millions of years. There was no need whatsoever for Him to have started the Creation five days before the creation of Adam and Eve. I have to believe that such a schedule would have required the use a tremendous amount of priesthood power. Though I believe He could have done it, I don't think it is God's style. God would have planted the seed, watered the earth, and waited for His creation to bloom.

Speaking of the beginning of the universe, Steven Hawking in *A Brief History of Time* stated,

> God, being omnipotent, could have started the universe off any way he wanted. . . . Yet it appears that he chose to make it evolve in a very regular way according to certain laws. It therefore seems equally reasonable to suppose that there are also laws governing the initial state.[6]

Dr. Hawking makes a good point. Shouldn't we expect the God we have come to know in the scriptures—patient and frugal with His power—to have created the universe and the world with patience and through natural means?

THE FOSSIL RECORD

Let us turn our attention to fossils. You can find fossils in most museums and, if you are lucky, on a hike in the wilderness. If you take all the fossils that have ever been found, you have what is called the fossil record. The fossil record is very strong evidence of evolution—simply because there is so much of it. Since fossils are usually made out of rock, there are, quite literally, thousands of tons of evidence in the fossil record. Museums across the world are filled with fossils. They are so plentiful that museums do not feel the need to preserve them all. You can buy your own fossils at most rock shops and museum gift stores for a small price.

There are two pieces of information that a fossil gives you. First, if you have the petrified remains of a complete skeleton, you can determine the general appearance of the animal or plant from which it came. Often, that animal or plant is no longer found on the earth. By far, the most well-known fossils of extinct animals are those of the dinosaurs. Re-creation of the skeletons of dinosaurs such as the *Tyrannosaurus Rex* and *Diplodocus* are main attractions at many museums. But dinosaurs are not the only animals to have become extinct. In the history of the world, there have been ten major mass extinctions.[7] Their causes were varied and are still under debate, but most appear to be related to climate change.

During each of these mass extinctions, between 50% and 95% of all species of flora and fauna, marine life or land life died out. So the diversity of plant and animal life you see on the earth today is a small fraction of all the species that have lived on the earth since its creation. Thousands of species of plants and animals have had the time to evolve, survive long enough to leave skeletons, and then die out. Such an enormous task would have required time—lots of time. This is but one of many arguments against the Young Earth creationist argument that the earth is less than 10,000 years old.

CARBON DATING

The second piece of information that fossils give you is their age. Some fairly impressive technology had to be developed to arrive at such dating, as fossils didn't give up their age easily. The first and most well-known of these technologies is carbon dating. Carbon-14, a radioisotope of the carbon-12 that makes up much of your body, is created when cosmic rays interact with atmospheric nitrogen. Much of that carbon-14 eventually ends up in a molecule of carbon dioxide, some of which is incorporated into plants by photosynthesis and into animals when they eat those plants. When the plant or animal dies, the amount of carbon-14 and carbon-12 in it are set, as no more intake of either will occur. However, over time the radioactive carbon-14 in the skeleton will decay back to its more stable form of Nitrogen-14. Exactly one-half of the carbon-14 in an animal's skeleton will decay every 5,730 years. Thus, the less carbon-14 is found in a bone, the older it is. Carbon dating was developed in 1946 by Willard F. Libby at the University of Chicago. The analysis can only accurately assess the ages of wood and other organic material that are less than 50,000 years old. But this range is certainly large enough to significantly influence discussions about the age of the earth.[8] Since its development, carbon-14 dating has been tested on many articles of known age—from the wood found in tombs of Egyptian pharaohs to the inner tree rings of very old trees.[9] Its dating has also been verified by checking it against other analytical methods, such as dendrochronology (determining the age of trees from their pattern of tree rings), varve chronology (determining the age of dig sites by the pattern of sedimentary layers in rock), and tephrochronology (determining age by matching the volcanic eruption ash presence to eruptions of known dates). Carbon dating has passed every test and challenge put to it. Despite some rather desperate attempts to discredit the technology by those who don't want to believe its results, its accuracy is well established.

Because the fossil record evidence is so strong, there have been numerous attempts to explain it away. One theory was that God, in constructing the earth, used parts of older planets and that is where such old fossils came from. This theory has been largely discredited, since many similar fossils come from sites within the same earth layer, but many hundreds of miles away from each other.

THERE IS A CONTROVERSY ONLY IF YOU ARE LOOKING FOR CONTROVERSY

There are many faithful believers in God who love Him very much. In general, these same people also love the scriptures and the inspiration and comfort that they provide. It is well known that if you love something, you protect it. Any attack, perceived or real, is defended against with passion and fervor.

Thus it has been with God and the scriptures. Science and evolution have been used to attack the Biblical rendering of the Creation and the existence of God Himself. In response, many of the faithful have responded with a stubborn defense. Compromise has been portrayed as a denial of one's testimony and of turning away from God and the scriptures. But accepting the possibility of altering one's beliefs in the light of new evidence is vital to growth. As a warning to those who take the extreme positions for or against evolution, Henry Eyring stated,

> I believe that many of our young people have impoverished their lives
> by a thoughtless denial of all aspects of the faith of their fathers in
> their desire to be what they call scientific and objective. Now I am also
> of the opinion that some theologians have unwittingly assisted in this
> rebellion by taking positions so dogmatic as to stifle the honest and
> thoughtful inquiries of youth when they need help and sought it.[10]

Creationists are ridiculed today because they refuse to consider the data—from astronomy, geology, biology, genetics, analytical chemistry, and other fields of science. They are in denial of the evidence. For example, the "Big Bang" model of the universe is now astronomy's standard model for the beginning of the universe.[11] Such a title means that most everyone who works in the field has accepted the Big Bang as truth. It is not a theory any more than Copernicus's conclusion that the earth revolves around the sun is still a theory. Evolution is not considered a theory anymore either. Those biologists, medical doctors, geneticists, chemists and paleontologists who work in this field have accepted evolution as truth. There is simply too much data supporting it to classify it as anything else.

As previously mentioned, in 1530, Nicolas Copernicus proposed that the earth revolved around the sun. This conclusion contradicted the idea that, since man was the greatest of God's creations, the earth was the center of the universe. The Catholic Church feared that this new theory would cause church members to lose their faith in God and cause the collapse of the church itself. So the church fought the concept at every step. Even the famous Galileo Galilei, an Italian astronomer who made many of the first observations of our solar system, was forced to renounce all belief in Copernicus's theories and was then sentenced to imprisonment for the rest of his life. In 1600, another astronomer of the time, Giordano Bruno, was reportedly tried, condemned, and burned at the stake for teaching the findings of Copernicus. But data was data, truth was truth, and the truth eventually won out. As we know, the Catholic Church was wrong—not only for its oppression of progressive astronomers of the time but also for thinking that the faithful would lose their faith simply because they learned a new fact about how the universe worked. Copernicus's model of the solar system did not cause the collapse of the Catholic Church, despite its fears to the contrary.

Likewise today, the discovery of the Big Bang and evolution will not cause faithful members to lose their testimonies. Neither discovery challenges the existence of God; it just gives us insight into His methods of creation. Our discoveries will not change the gospel, though it may cause us to change our understanding of that same gospel. Though we may learn that some of what we learned in Primary class is not quite accurate, those new insights actually make stronger testimonies. Understanding how God created the universe and life does not take away from His grandeur.

So let us now move our discussion from the creation of a single planet to the creation of a whole universe. The beginning of the universe is certainly part of the Creation story. If science can find complexity and wonder in this event, it can yet again build our faith in the back-stage direction of a Creator.

NOTES

1. "Creationism," Dictionary.com, accessed April 4, 2017 http://dictionary.com/browse/creationism.

2. Frances Collins, *The Language of God*, (New York: Free Press, 2006), 152.

3. Henry Eyring, *The Faith of a Scientist* (Salt Lake City: Bookcraft).

4. John A. Widtsoe, *Joseph Smith as a Scientist* (Eborn Books, 1908), 52.

5. Ibid., 57.

6. Stephen Hawking, *A Brief History of Time*, (Bantam Books, 1996), 11.

7. Stephen Jay Gould, *The Book of Life* (New York: W. W. Norton, 1993), 106–109.

8. Doug MacDougall, *Nature's Clocks* (Berkeley: University of California Press, 2008).

9. David Montgomery, *The Rocks Don't Lie* (New York: W. W. Norton, 2012), 192.

10. Eyring, *The Faith of a Scientist*, 31.

11. Steven Weinberg, *The First Three Minutes* (New York: Basic Books, 1988), 4.

4

THE BIG BANG AND
OUR UNIVERSE

Sometimes, to understand the reasons for your life and destiny, you have to look back to the very beginning. The creation of the universe was the very first step in a process that took billions of years and led to our lives on this earth. It was, quite literally, the beginning of time and matter.

There have been a number of models proposed to explain how the universe began. In 1929, the Big Bang became one of those models. Data collected by Edwin Hubble showed conclusively that our neighboring galaxies were all moving away from us at impressive speeds. How is this possible? Though it is a somewhat flawed analogy, think of a limp balloon, upon which you draw a number of separate dots. Now, blow up your balloon. All the dots move further away from each other. So, in an expanding universe, one can visualize galaxies all moving away from each other. But the universe would have to have a center, or its starting point. If you look toward an explosion after you hear it, you can tell by the direction of the dust and debris thrown into the air where the explosion occurred. Similarly, if you look at the directions and speeds of the galaxies around us and plot them on a three-dimensional universe map, you can tell about where the Big Bang occurred. If you know the speeds that the galaxies have been receding from each other over that space, you can also approximate when the Big Bang occurred (about 14 billion years ago). Since 1929, astronomers have been observing the receding galaxies and plotting their paths. The data is overwhelming in its support of the Big Bang model of the Creation and expansion of the universe.

It is a huge understatement to call the Big Bang an explosion. Explosions are simply reactions that expand gases so quickly that a shock wave develops, blowing away any matter in its path. The Big Bang was such a vast burst of energy that it first created all the matter in the universe and only then blew that matter out into the universe. Before the Big Bang occurred, there was no matter, nor space, nor time in our universe. This is nearly incomprehensible. We generally think of space and time to be infinite. How could there have been a "time" when neither existed? Since there was no matter yet, there were no physical laws yet in place to govern that matter. On an atomic scale, there were no atoms and, thus, no nuclear forces to hold those atoms together. On an astronomic scale, there were no suns or planets—and thus no gravity to hold them together. In the moment of the Big Bang, not only were staggering amounts of energy and matter created, the laws that govern that energy and matter were also set. The strength of gravity that holds suns, planets, and galaxies together was established, as was the strength of the forces that hold atoms together. Speaking of the size, mass, and forces that hold atoms together and that hold planets, suns, and galaxies together in their orbits, Sir Martin Rees observed, "And everything takes place in the arena of an expanding universe, whose properties were imprinted at the time of the initial Big Bang."[1]

Few of us tend to think that the constants and equations that we learned about in physics class were part of the Creation. But they were. When a universe is created, the laws which govern that universe and literally hold it together have to be established. Otherwise that universe would immediately collapse into disorder and chaos. To complicate the establishment of these laws even more, if the universe was going to be a place for humans to evolve and grow, those constants and equations must eventually come together in a way to support life. The complexity of such a task is enormous. Francis Collins summarizes, "The Big Bang cries out for a divine explanation. It forces the conclusion that nature had a defined beginning. I cannot see how nature could have created itself.

Only a supernatural force that is outside of space and time could have done that."[2]

But before launching into an examination of the technical features of the Big Bang, one should stop and consider the reasons behind it. Why did the Big Bang occur? Since it created all the "matter unorganized" in the universe, a more philosophical way to ask this same question is, "Why is there something instead of nothing?" Though there are many books on how the Big Bang occurred, few of them consider the *why* of it, with good reason. Such a question leads to a discussion about the metaphysical, religion, and God, topics about which astronomers and physicists are neither comfortable nor generally adept at discussing. But the astrophysicist Stephen Hawking took a shot at it. In his best-selling book, *A Brief History of Time*, Hawking wrote, "It would be very difficult to explain why the universe should have begun in just this way, except as the act of a God who intended to create beings like us."[3]

But we can leave the discussion of why we exist for another time. Really, the major question before us is, "Who brought it to pass?" One answer is God; the other is random events. The following is a list of the constants and physical laws of nature that were established at the moment of the Big Bang. We will learn that the Big Bang was a very precisely programmed event to provide us a universe that would evolve over billions of years to support life.

THE TOTAL MATTER AND FORCE CREATED BY THE BIG BANG

The energy put into the Big Bang had to be immense yet controlled. First, it had to be a large enough release of energy to create all the matter in the universe. From Einstein's $E=mc^2$ equation, we know that it takes a lot of energy to make a little bit of matter. No adjective is sufficient to describe the amount of energy required to make enough matter to fill a universe. Incredibly, that conversion of energy to matter all occurred just a few seconds after the "detonation." Not only did the Big Bang create matter, it put enough kinetic energy behind it to send it flying into space for billions of years. If the explosion had been too small, all of that newly-created matter would have not been dispersed enough. Gravity, pulling in from the larger amount of matter in the core of the universe, would have been able to stop all outward motion of the expanding universe and then pulled everything back to collapse into an immense black hole at the starting point. But if the explosion had been too great, all the matter created would have been dispersed so widely that gravity could never have pulled enough localized matter together to create galaxies, suns, and planets. The universe would have been a large space with gasses floating about. As you might guess, neither option is conducive to life . . .

There is another way to look at this concept. More matter creates more gravity. Thus, the amount of matter created in the Big Bang had to be balanced with the force of the explosion. In summary, the Big Bang had to create the right amount of matter, give it the right amount of gravity, and send it hurtling out into the expanding universe with the right amount of speed. Such intricate, foresightful programming is impressive.

THE DEUTERIUM BOTTLENECK

As noted earlier, much of the energy of the Big Bang was converted into matter. Since it is the smallest and simplest element, most all of that original matter was created in the form of hydrogen. Hydrogen is the primary fuel for all the suns in the universe. In a sun's core, hydrogen fuses to become helium, a reaction that emits huge amounts of energy. As one can well imagine, the Big Bang was very, very hot. Hotter than the core of even the largest sun, the Big Bang caused temperatures of 100 billion degrees Celsius at its core.[4] Nuclear reactions, like chemical reactions, go faster at higher temperatures. At these temperatures, the nuclear fusion reactions that convert hydrogen to helium are really easy to maintain. In fact, at these temperatures, there was a danger that all of the hydrogen could have been converted to helium in the first seconds of the Big Bang. This would have exhausted the supply of hydrogen that was needed to fuel billions of suns for billions of years.

For a hydrogen nuclei (which has one proton) to become a helium nuclei (which has two protons and two neutrons), it must first form into a deuterium nuclei (which has one proton and one neutron). Fortunately, deuterium is unstable at high temperatures. For the first three minutes after the Big Bang, deuterium nuclei formed rapidly, but then broke down again to hydrogen nuclei just as fast. Deuterium simply could not endure the high temperatures of those first few seconds after time and space began. After nearly four minutes, the expanding universe was "cool" enough (though still at 0.9 billion °C) for deuterium to exist long enough to be converted to helium. The nuclear fission reactions that converted hydrogen nuclei to helium nuclei occurred at full throttle for the next 30 minutes or so, converting about 25% of all hydrogen into helium. But during those 30 minutes the universe expanded incredibly, dropping its pressure and temperature. The temperature of the new universe had dropped to 0.3 billion °C and a much lower pressure, below that needed to sustain the hydrogen fusion reaction.[4] Helium concentrations leveled off at about 25% of all matter, with the rest being mostly hydrogen. So, the universe still had plenty of hydrogen to fuel its future suns. We can either give credit to a Creator for programming the hydrogen fusion reaction of the Big Bang with a deuterium bottleneck such that all of our sun's fuel was not burned up within seconds or give credit elsewhere.

Continuing our narrative, about 700,000 years later, temperatures had dropped to the point where electrons could join with the hydrogen and helium nuclei and form atoms. The mass of these atoms exerted their tiny amounts of gravity on each other and began to coalesce.

THE FORMATION OF GALAXIES

I would like you to picture a firework. Generally a firework will explode straight out and the sparks that light up the sky are very evenly distributed within the globe of the explosion. That is the way most of us might picture the Big Bang as well. The greatest explosion in the history of the universe would be expected to spray its matter and energy equally in all directions, wouldn't it? But if matter had been distributed equally in all of space, how would gravity been able to pull galaxies together? Any particle, gaseous or otherwise, would have been pulled in all directions at once. No coalescence could have occurred. If there had not been areas in the expanding universe of denser matter, there would have been no centers for galaxies to form around.

So, the Big Bang was more of a shaped charge, designed to be asymmetrical and send more gaseous matter in certain directions than others. These gases in the highest density centers coalesced to form galaxies, suns, solar systems, and a few habitable planets. Our own Milky Way galaxy formed in a location far enough away from other galaxies to not be threatened by their gravity or radiation. The Big Bang was not a simple explosion, but an intricately designed expansion that would allow the formation of new galaxies habitable for life for billions of years to come.

THE FORCE OF GRAVITY
AND THE BIRTH OF SUNS

Gravity is an attractive force between two bodies of matter. In the Big Bang, the amount of gravitational force per kilogram of matter was established for this universe. As noted, when the universe was young, the strength of gravity was instrumental in bringing together matter to forms suns, planets and galaxies.

Gravity is, of course, still key for the universe to function. Holding us on the surface of the earth is just one of its tasks that we should appreciate. For example, gravity is also essential for suns to shine. Before a sun "ignites" it is a globe of collapsing nebula made up of two gases—hydrogen and helium. Over time, gravity pulls the gas atoms in closer and closer together. This causes an ever-increasing number of atomic collisions, which give off energy. Temperatures rise, leading to more collisions and more heat. The globe of gas tries to expand as temperatures increase, but gravity is relentless and continues to pull the gas atoms together. Finally, the pressure and temperatures wrought by gravity becomes so great that they overcome the atomic forces that hold atoms apart. Fusion of hydrogen into helium begins to occur and the equivalent energy of numerous atomic bombs is released in the center of the new sun. After our sun ignited, internal temperatures eventually stabilized at about 15,000,000 degrees Celsius.[5] Such tremendous heat violently pushes the gaseous atoms apart from each other and the sun expands.

If gravity stopped functioning at this point, the sun would self-destruct with a massive explosion. The sun's mass would be shot out into the heavens and, without the pressures and temperatures needed to drive the fusion reaction, the sun's radiance would be quickly extinguished. But gravity does not stop and the sun is not allowed to destroy itself. Gravity maintains its grip on the gases within the sun and the outward expansion caused by the first atomic reactions is halted. Eventually, equilibrium is reached. The high temperatures from the fusion reactions occurring in the center of the sun continue to try to expand it. But gravity holds the sun together, maintaining the temperature and pressures needed for fusion reactions to continue. Our sun has been radiating the energy needed for life on this planet for about 4.5 billion years and is slated to continue for another 4.5 billion more. Suns are an amazing and absolutely critical feature of our universe. So, the next time you feel the warmth of the sun on your face, thank gravity. Better yet, thank the God who established gravity in our universe in the first place.

Besides its other duties, gravity keeps the planets in their orbits and our moon in the night sky. It keeps us secured to the ground. It was one of the most important parameters established at the Big Bang.

CARBON AND OXYGEN

Thus far into the Creation narrative, essentially all of the matter in the universe is made up of hydrogen and helium, some of which has coalesced into a large number of suns. Obviously, we are going to need some heavier elements such as iron, nickel, silica, and magnesium to create our planet; nitrogen and oxygen to give it an atmosphere; and carbon on which to base all life forms. To make these heavier elements, one needs raw material, such as hydrogen and helium, very high temperatures, and very high pressures. Fortunately, these materials and conditions all happen to be found in the middle of suns, especially very old suns. During a sun's lifetime, it will begin to form some heavier elements in its core. But the real production occurs after the sun has aged, which is defined as the time that the sun starts to run out of its primary fuel. As a sun runs out of its hydrogen, fusion reactions slow. Temperatures start to drop in its core. Without the immense heat to push its atoms apart, the sun begins to shrink again due to gravity. This collapse raises pressures and temperatures again until the central temperature again starts to rise. Though the star is running low on hydrogen to fuse, it now has a great deal of helium. At these increased pressures and temperatures, it is helium's turn to fuse.

A helium atom can fuse with a hydrogen atom to produce lithium, a solid element used in the production of batteries. A helium atom can also fuse with another helium atom to produce beryllium. At first, both of these elements are very unstable and decay almost instantly. But temperatures continue to build and more beryllium is made. Once beryllium is produced faster than it can decay, the amount of beryllium in the stellar core increases. Beryllium atoms are then able to fuse with helium atoms to form carbon. Carbon is the building block of life. Without carbon we would not exist. So, fortunately for us, carbon is quite stable and starts to build up higher concentrations in the suns hellish environment.

If you were paying attention, you noticed that the production of carbon requires that three helium nuclei collide and stick together. But nuclei are very small and such a lucky occurrence is very unlikely. Thus, one might expect carbon to be a very rare element. However, as it turns out, beryllium, helium, and their carbon product all have almost exactly the same vibration energy. Somewhat like three tuning forks, the three elements resonate, greatly increasing the probability that the beryllium atom will successfully combine with hydrogen to form carbon.

As stated, carbon is quite stable, but as the star ages some carbon atoms can fuse with additional helium atoms to produce oxygen. The oxygen thus produced is also quite stable. As the star continues to collapse, some of the carbon and oxygen will continue to fuse to create larger atoms such as the minerals and metals that will be needed to create planets. But, due to their stability, only a fraction of these two elements is converted into the heavier elements. This is very fortunate for us as we need a lot of both carbon and oxygen to create organic life. The fusion reactions that occur in the middle of suns to give us the elements of the periodic table are very complex. But these reactions are seemingly programmed to give us all the elements we need to create a world and fill it with life.

LAWS OF PHYSICS
THAT ALLOW LIFE

In this chapter, we have only considered a few examples of how the Big Bang was structured to create a universe that could support life. We have not discussed the other physical constants, all established at the Big Bang, that are crucial to the development of life. In his book *Just Six Numbers*, Martin Rees describes these constants of energy and matter, including the force that holds atomic nuclei together, the electrical forces that hold atoms together, the relative strength of antigravity and gravity, the change gravity experiences with distance, and even the fact that there are three dimensions in our universe. Had any of those numbers varied slightly from their chosen values, life would not exist. Frances Collins recognized several more constants of extreme importance.

> Altogether, there are fifteen physical constants whose values current theory is unable to predict. They are givens: they simply have the value that they have. This list includes the speed of light, the strength of the weak and strong nuclear forces, various parameters associated with electromagnetism, and the force of gravity. The chance that all of these constants would take on the values necessary to result in a stable universe capable of sustaining complex life forms is almost infinitesimal.[6]

It is not just a happy coincidence or incredible luck that the Big Bang created the gases that would fuse in the center of suns to make up the elements that would eventually allow the formation of the planets where life could be born. God organized the Big Bang, initiated it, and controlled it to produce the material and space with which to continue His acts of creation. His direction was, however, purposefully behind the scenes and thus not immediately apparent to many.

But, even with these proofs, the belief that God initiated the creation of the universe will almost certainly remain a matter of faith. We have no scriptures on the subject. Genesis 1:1 starts with the creation of the earth, about ten billion years after the creation of the universe. God has never displayed a willingness to reveal anything on the subject in latter-day revelation. And it is very unlikely that science will shed any more light on the subject. The Big Bang was a "singularity," meaning it happened once and only once in the history of the universe. So we won't be seeing another one and, since scientists cannot simulate the conditions present during the Big Bang expansion, experimentation is not viable. We are learning what we can from the universe as we see it today, which is all we can do.

OUR SOLAR SYSTEM

To continue our Creation story, once the physical laws of nature were established, the universe expanded. Suns were formed, they aged, and then many exploded. In essence, the universe proceeded on its programmed course for about 10 billion years. Inside a distant corner of the galaxy now called the Milky Way, a gigantic cloud of dust and gas, called a nebula, hovered. It is believed that the explosion of a supernova pushed some of the cloud back into itself, causing an area of higher density matter. Gravity asserted itself, and the densest center started pulling dust and gasses in from the rest of the cloud. Two things then happened. First, a sphere of gasses and dust formed in the center of the cloud. (Every sun and planet is a sphere because it is the most efficient way for gravity to pack matter around a central point.) But some of the cloud was moving before the nebula had started pulling it in, possibly due to the shock wave of the supernova. That movement, called angular momentum, caused that material to start a spiral around the middle sphere. Gravity prevented this moving matter from escaping the newly-forming solar system, but the angular momentum prevented it from plummeting into the center.

But all this material circling the sun had to align. Like ice skaters circling a frozen pond, the rocks and dust bumped and collided to get everything flowing in the same general direction. This caused the nebula cloud to flatten into a large disk with a bulge in the center. Like one of the better skaters on our pond spins faster as she draws her hands in closer to her body, the disk spun faster as it contracted. At some point, in a process already described, our center bulge ignited to become our sun. The heat from that ignition immediately melted the frozen gases close to it, leaving only the rocks and heavier elements there. The frozen hydrogen and helium gasses far enough away from the sun to not feel the heat or shock wave were unaffected.

Gravity continued pulling pieces together and the rocky material in the inner orbits to the sun started coming together to form larger rocks. Gradually, Mercury, Venus, Earth, and Mars took shape and grew by pulling in all the debris close to their orbits. The gas giants Jupiter, Saturn, Uranus, and Neptune were also formed by pulling in the scattered gasses and a few heavier elements from their orbits. Some of the space between Mars and Jupiter was not cleared out very well and is now called our asteroid belt. Our nebula had become a solar system with one sun and eight planets, including Earth (but not Pluto).

NOTES

1. Martin Reese, *Just Six Numbers* (New York: Basic Books, 2000), 1.
2. Frances Collins, *The Language of God* (New York, Free Press, 2006), 67.
3. Stephen Hawking, *A Brief History of Time* (New York: Bantam Books, 1988), 131.
4. Steven Weinberg, *The First Three Minutes* (New York: Basic Books, 1988), 102–112.
5. John Gribbin, *The Birth of Time* (London: Orion Books, 1999), 40.
6. Collins, *The Language of God*, 74.

5

THE EARTH

So, the Big Bang provided us with our universe, which included a galaxy called the Milky Way. Within that galaxy, a nebula space cloud of matter came together to form our solar system. The third planet out from the sun in that solar system was our planet Earth. It was now time to put some life into that planet.

But life has a large number of requirements of a planet before it can take up residence there. We humans are an especially fragile species, and we impose an even larger number of requirements on our planet for us to be able to survive. Earth had to be optimal in every aspect, of course, or we would not be here. This chapter is dedicated to describing characteristics of our solar system and Earth that are necessary for the development and sustaining of life. As with the descriptions of the Big Bang and the formation of our universe, we can attribute these favorable attributes to very good luck or to God. In any case, the Earth is a much more complex place than we often appreciate. So let us review just a few of Earth's attributes which allow us to live here.

EARTH HAD TO SPIN ON ITS AXIS

How does a round sun provide continued warmth and energy to a round planet on a continuous basis? There is only one way—you have to rotate the planet so all of its sides get a chance to face its sun. If the planet is not rotating, each hemisphere has to face the sun for half of its year and be in darkness for the other half. The temperature swings of such a situation are severe. Our best local example of this is the planet Mercury, which rotates only once every 59 Earth days. Mercury also has no atmosphere to modulate temperatures like Earth. With that deficiency and its slow rotation, the parts of Mercury facing the sun can have surface temperatures of over 800°F. During its month-long night, temperatures can drop down to less than -250°F. Life cannot survive such temperatures.

Fortunately, the Earth was set on a rotation that allows all parts of the planet both enough time to warm and time to cool over each 24-hour cycle. That spin gives us light in which to work and darkness in which to sleep. Finally, the Earth's spin is critical to sustaining its magnetic field that protects us from solar wind and cosmic rays.

EARTH HAD TO HAVE A MAGNETIC FIELD

The North and South Poles were so named because every magnet has one of each and Earth is a very large magnet. The process by which Earth's magnetic field is produced is very complex. The inner core of the earth is a solid ball of nickel-iron alloy. The outer core of the Earth, extending from 1,800 to 3,200 miles beneath our feet, is mostly hot (5000 °C), semi-liquid iron.[1] Due to both the Earth's rotation and convection heating, this magma moves through and around the solid, nickel-iron inner core of our planet. This movement builds charges, which induce a stable electrical current to form in the magma. The electric current causes a magnetic field to form within the core, and the two build upon one another. Our planet's spin causes the magma to spiral in the same direction, further aligning and strengthening the magnetic fields. As anyone who has played with a magnet can tell you, a magnetic force extends beyond the magnet itself. The magnetic field of Earth, called our magnetosphere, extends miles out into space. Not only does that magnetic field allow compasses to function and migrating birds to know where to fly, this field has more life-sustaining properties as well.

Along with the warming rays of sunshine, the earth is bombarded with a steady stream of high energy particles (mostly electrons, protons and alpha particles). Some of these particles come from the sun and are called the solar wind. Others are from outer space and are known as cosmic rays. These high-energy particles are very similar to the particles emitted by a radioactive substance. Though of a lower intensity, being under a continuous shower of such radiation every day would cause increased levels of cancer, DNA damage, birth defects, and radiation sickness. Unprotected from such radiation, life almost certainly could never have attained its foothold on our planet.

Fortunately, the Earth's magnetic field shields our planet from most of these particles. Most of these high-energy particles are charged. When they encounter the Earth's magnetic field, they are deflected (similar to the deflection of water around the bow of a ship) to fly harmlessly into space. The few particles that do make it through the magnetosphere are prevented from getting to us by our atmosphere. Who would have guessed that a process that occurs in the core of our earth and gives us the North and South poles also protects our lives and allows us to thrive on our planet?

EARTH HAD TO BE IN THE RIGHT NEIGHBORHOOD

Our galaxy, rather poetically called "The Milky Way," is one of about 100 billion galaxies within the visible universe. Ours is a spiral galaxy, so named due to its flat structure with multiple arms that spiral away from the core. Our solar system is located about two-thirds of the way from the center to the edge of the galaxy, in a rather empty space between two of those arms. Our nearest neighboring star is Alpha Centauri, which is 4.3 light-years away.

Our remote galactic neighborhood is a good choice in which to raise a family, or life of any kind. Closer to the core of the Milky Way, there is a much denser packing of suns and supernovae. These are all sources of intense cosmic radiation from which not even our magnetosphere or atmosphere could protect us. In the more crowded areas of our galaxy, life as we know it could have never survived the constant radiation onslaught from surrounding suns. Even if we could teleport there today, depending on where we landed, we would soon succumb to radiation sickness, sterility, and several forms of cancer. Early life would probably have never had a chance.

If we lived on a planet closer to the galactic core and the radiation didn't kill us, gravitational attractions to nearby suns or giant planets would have almost certainly pulled Earth's orbit out of the circular orbit around the sun that we now enjoy. Such jostling of Earth's orbit would have pulled us closer and then further away from our sun. The resulting swings in Earth's temperature and climate would have made life on our planet impossible.[2]

Yet we couldn't have been on the very fringes of the galaxy either. Since there are very few suns and supernovae in that region to produce elements beyond hydrogen and helium, there are probably few planets. The few rocky planets that have formed are very likely metal poor and would not be expected to have the iron and other heavy metals so necessary for an industrial society. Thus, our location in the galaxy was a good selection.

OUR SUN HAD TO BE THE RIGHT AGE AND SIZE

Our sun is the right age. It is not so young that it is still going through the violent stages of a newly formed sun with massive solar flares and devastating solar winds. Yet it is not so old that it is starting to burn out and reduce its light output. Our star is middle-aged. It has shone steadily for at about 4.5 billion years and should be good for several billion more.

Our sun is also the right size for us. It is not so big and hot that we would require a much larger orbit to survive, resulting in overly long summers and winters. Yet it is not so small that we would need to be very close to it to be able to collect enough energy for life.

EARTH HAD TO BE
THE RIGHT SIZE

Next, our Earth is the right size. If Earth were as large as Jupiter, its gravity would crush us. If Earth were as small as the moon, we would float more than walk, and, much worse, it would not have enough gravity to hold an atmosphere in place.

THE RIGHT DISTANCE
FROM THE SUN

There is a region of space that is not too cold (too far from the sun) and not too hot (too close to the sun) to support life. This region is called, appropriately, the Goldilocks Zone, because this region of space is not too hot and not too cold. As the fairytale name implies, this zone is just right. But the Goldilocks Zone is pretty small. If Earth was just 5% closer to the sun, we would be on the inner edge of the habitable zone. We have a little more room on the outside edge. We could be 70% further from the sun and still survive. This is approximately where Mars is located, which has given us some hope for its colonization in the distant future. But we could only possibly live there with state-of-the-art NASA technology and supplies from Earth, including air, water, food, energy, and shelter. Mars has an average temperature of -80°F, and it is extremely unlikely that life could have evolved there. Even with our technologies that might make Mars survivable, it could never support a significant population on its own.

A ROUND ORBIT

Fortunately, Earth's orbit around the sun is very round, with a total variation of only 3%. But that is not the case with many planets, whose elliptical orbits take them closer and then further away from the sun. This causes swings in temperature that most life could not endure. Mars is our closest and best example, averaging 228 million kilometers from the sun. But its elliptical orbit causes it to range from 10% closer to 10% further away. With the same variation to our own orbit, our planet as a whole would have very hot summers (putting us outside of our Goldilocks Zone) and much colder winters. In general, life prefers moderate temperatures, which explains why there is less life in the desert and polar regions than elsewhere on the earth. Thus a circular orbit, allowing controlled and moderate temperatures, has been an essential aspect of life.

THE MOON

There are theories that the moon was needed to allow evolution to occur. One of the most notable transitions of evolution had to be in going from life in the ocean to life on land. Tides may have had a role in that transition by providing an area along the coasts that was underwater for only part of the day. Though logical, it is hard to say if the tides actually affected our evolutionary path.

However, the moon certainly has a stabilizing effect on the rotation of the Earth. Comparing Earth to Mars yet again, like a slowly spinning top, our neighboring planet has wobbled quite dramatically around its axis over time. The wobble caused the ice that was once at the poles on Mars to drift to what was once its equator. But the beginning of such a wobble by Earth is fought by the Moon's gravity, stabilizing our axis of rotation and keeping it pointed in the same direction. As a result, Earth has had much less climatic change over the millennia than it would have had without a moon. Like many of our examples, this has changed the way life evolved on Earth. It allowed for the emergence of more complex organisms compared to a planet where drastic climatic change would have either prevented life or limited it to only simpler, though probably much hardier, organisms.

The moon has helped stabilize Earth's climate in other ways. The ocean tides help transport heat from the equator to the poles and encourage the mixing of the deep ocean. The moon, large enough to create the tides but not big enough or close enough to cause the shifting of landmasses, has been an important asset to life.

JUPITER

Jupiter is the largest planet in our solar system and, believe it or not, has been a factor in allowing life to develop on Earth. First, Jupiter is not so close to us that it can destabilize our orbit around the sun. Second, there is a large ring of asteroids that is between the orbits of Mars and Jupiter. Those asteroids have never been able to coalesce into a large planet that could disrupt Earth's orbit because the gravitational forces of Jupiter tear them apart. As long as the asteroids in the belt stay small, Jupiter cannot pull them into itself. But if a number of those asteroids, through their own gravitational attraction, start to form a larger body, then Jupiter pulls the growing mass in toward itself and away from us.

Jupiter is also a "sink" for meteors and asteroids. Sixty-five million years ago, a huge meteorite crashed near the town of Chicxulub on the Yucatan peninsula and, it is believed, caused the extinction of most of our favorite dinosaurs. While the extinction of the dinosaurs may have helped in the evolution of mammals and mankind, we are very blessed that such large meteorite strikes aren't a more common occurrence, since they tend to have devastating effects on life. Millions of organisms die and thousands of species are driven to extinction. So, why don't we see more large and destructive meteorites hitting Earth? Because most of them, whether meteors entering our solar system or asteroids orbiting in their belt, feel the tug of Jupiter's gravity long before that of our tiny Earth. The potentially dangerous space rocks respond to those tugs and adjust their trajectory toward Jupiter. The meteor either crashes into Jupiter or, if it has the speed, rushes past it. But, in either case, the space rock is pulled away from us. As one might expect, meteorite collisions with Jupiter are not uncommon. The latest observed impact on Jupiter was detected in July 2009. The impact before that was of the Shoemaker-Levy 9 comet in July of 1994.

A BREATHABLE ATMOSPHERE

For the first half of its life, Earth had little to no oxygen in its atmosphere. Only anaerobic bacteria, which prefer not to have oxygen around, existed. But then some of these bacteria, ancestors of our present-day cyanobacteria, evolved a way to take energy from sunlight and use it to make sugars from water and carbon dioxide. The by-product of that photosynthesis was oxygen. As explained by Martin Rees in *Just Six Numbers*, "Our Earth's atmosphere is rich in oxygen; it didn't start out that way, but was transformed by primitive bacteria in its early history . . . For a billion years, primitive organisms exhaled oxygen, transforming the young Earth's atmosphere and clearing the way for multicellular life."[3]

For 200 million years, all the oxygen produced by cyanobacteria was chemically captured and bound up by dissolved iron, other metals, and organic matter. But the cyanobacteria population kept growing and, in what is now known as the Great Oxygenation Event, oxygen started accumulating in the atmosphere. Organisms that needed oxygen to live (i.e., just about everything in the animal kingdom, including us) could now evolve. Yet one more step critical to life was taken.

WATER

All life depends on water. Every living organism on our planet needs water. Bacteria, algae, fish, and other sea creatures live in it. Over half of your body and about 92% of your blood is made up of water. If cut off from all sustenance, you will die of dehydration long before you will starve. Even in the driest desert, life must have water. Water even plays a major role in the Creation story. All of Day Two (Genesis 1:6–8) and part of Day Three (Genesis 1:9–10) are spent getting water to the right places.

Not only does water have to exist, but it also has a list of very unique and very necessary characteristics of its own. For blood to flow through the small capillaries in our bodies and brains, water needs its low viscosity. For boats to float, water must have its high surface tension. For oceans to stabilize global temperatures, water has to have a high heat capacity. To supply oxygen to fish, allow cell chemistry to function, and distribute minerals and nutrients throughout all plants and animals, water must have its high solubilization capacity. Water is the only liquid that allows acids and enzymes to do their work so you can digest your food. If water was just a little different in structure or chemistry, it would fail at some of its many tasks, and life would not have occurred.

The list of the unique features of water continues. One property of water is especially obvious yet greatly underappreciated. Ice floats. We pretty much take that for granted, as we consider the ice cubes floating in our drinking glass. But that small fact allows marine life to occur in any part of the earth that has a winter. In most all other liquids, the solid, frozen forms are denser than the liquid, so its frozen form sinks. Ice is actually *less* dense than liquid water, which allows it to float. When lakes and seas freeze, they do so from the top down. As the ice forms on a lake's surface, it does not sink to the bottom, killing all the fish and plant life. Instead, the ice insulates what heat is still in the water. These two characteristics prevent our seas and lakes from freezing solid and killing all its seaweed and marine life. This one unique property of water preserves the fish and other marine life that are essential as food sources today. If ice didn't float, our planet would be much less habitable.

THE REQUIREMENTS OF ADVANCED CIVILIZATIONS

It can be argued that the following characteristics of Earth were not necessary for humanity's survival. But without them, it is doubtful that we would have ever attained the advanced civilization that we enjoy today.

WOOD

Trees are an incredible resource. Wood burns, so early man could use fire to keep himself warm, enabling him to live in the colder regions of our planet and survive the winters. Wood is sturdy and, if kept dry, does not rot away. Thus, since prehistoric times and yet today, wood has provided the structures for our homes and businesses. Wood floats. For millennia, wood has been used to build the boats that mankind has used to explore and colonize new lands, transport crops, and trade goods. Trees evolved from much smaller plants which allowed them to grow above their fellows and take in more sunlight. Such evolution did not necessarily have to occur, but it certainly helped mankind by doing so.

METALS

But wood could only take us so far. Metals have had such a significant effect on the progress of our civilization that early history is recorded according to the metal being used during that time for tools and weapons. Thus, following the Stone Age, we have the Bronze Age (from 3200 BC to 600 BC) and the Iron Age (from 1200 BC to 1 BC). The strength of steel has allowed the production of the tools needed to mine, dig for oil, plant and harvest thousands of square miles of crops, build skyscrapers, and manufacture trains, planes, and automobiles. Other metals are used by the electronics industry to make the circuit boards and chips used by our computers and cell phones. Without metals, we would have had to remain in the Stone Age. Again, there was no guarantee that our Earth would come with underground metal deposits just waiting for us to dig them up. Earth provides.

ENERGY—COAL, OIL, AND NATURAL GAS

Besides the materials we needed to build our shelters, tools, and transportation, mankind needed energy. We needed energy to heat millions of homes across the world and power the aforementioned trains, planes, and automobiles that transport us. These natural resources run the mills and manufacturing plants that produce our food, clothes, and everything else we own. Coal, oil, and natural gas are sources of concentrated energy, provided by our Earth, which allowed us to enter an Industrial Age. Most of these energy sources were produced by plant and animal life that sank to the bottom of oceans and other bodies of water. This organic debris was then covered by layers of earth that compressed and heated it over the millennia, converting it to petroleum, natural gas, and coal. Over millions of years our planet provided the conditions needed for the production of energy sources that we use today. Yet again, there is no rule that this process had to occur. What are the chances we should be so lucky?

THE BEAUTY OF EARTH

Finally, one could certainly argue that beauty was a characteristic of our Earth that was really unnecessary for man's survival. Beauty does not feed us, clothe us, or protect us from the elements. Nevertheless, we have a planet of awe-inspiring beauty. I have always considered the beauty of nature to be an over-the-top blessing that God added to His Creation to inspire men to treasure the earth and love our time here.

Science can explain each and every aspect of beauty that the universe and Earth offers. It is certainly true that flowers evolved to be colorful and fragrant to attract insects and birds to be vectors for the transfer of pollen. Butterflies and birds evolved their own colors to discourage predators, attract mates, and provide camouflage. We know that the reds and oranges of a beautiful sunset are caused by the increased scatter of the blue wavelengths of sunlight during its longer trip through the atmosphere. The four seasons of winter, spring, summer, and fall are caused by the 23.4° tilt of Earth to its axis of rotation around the sun. The green leaves of deciduous trees turn colors in the autumn because the shorter days trigger the tree to stop producing chlorophyll, which allows the yellow and orange carotenoids to show through. Mountain ranges are created when tectonic plates come together and one is pushed up above the other. The moon was a small planetoid that skimmed Earth when it was very young and was then captured by our planet's gravity. Stars are actually suns and galaxies that are light years away from us, whose light seems to twinkle because it has to pass through our atmosphere.

In summary, we can certainly explain away the beauty of nature and the universe with the functional reasons for beauty's existence. Some would tell you that such beauty is a happenstance of the Creation. But I am not one of those people. I believe the world is more beautiful than it had to be. Flowers, butterflies and birds, sunsets, fall colors, mountains, rainbows, or the moon and stars probably didn't need to be as

vibrantly colorful or as beautiful as they are to meet their assigned purpose or cause. God made the world especially beautiful for us, such that
we might have joy.

In another example of an over-the-top blessing, I believe God gave
us music such that we may *hear* beauty as well. Beautiful music does not
serve any evolutionary purpose of which I am aware. But it adds greatly
to our joy of living and God wanted us to have that blessing. This is a
deep-seated, personal opinion that I cannot prove. I have no evidence
that I can give for it. But I think it is implied in the scriptures.

In the Creation story given in Genesis 1, God observes that what
He had created was "good" *seven* times. Actually on the seventh time,
God seems to give Himself a little more credit. The last verse of the
chapter states, "And God saw every thing that he had made, and,
behold, it was very good." I believe that God has probably seen some
very beautiful places.

Thus, I believe that God has a pretty high standard for the word
"good" and the Earth had to be exceptionally beautiful to be given a
"very good" rating. There are undoubtedly some very impressive sights
in the rest of the universe. But, given the evidence, I don't expect them to
be any more beautiful than the views we have right here on the Earth. As
unscientific as it may sound, the sheer *beauty* of the universe, the Earth,
and life itself needs to be added to the list of proofs of God's design.
If you doubt this conclusion, maybe you should go outside and watch
the sunset.

Notes

1. "Earth's Interior," *National Geographic*, accessed May 15, 2018, http://
    science.nationalgeographic.com/science/earth/inside-the-earth.
2. Gerald L. Schroeder, *God According to God* (New York: Harper One,
    2009), 63–64.
3. Martin Rees, *Just Six Numbers* (New York: Basic Books, 2000), 19–20.

6

THE BEGINNINGS OF LIFE

I t is a tendency of mankind that, before we really understand something well, we tend to oversimplify it. So for many decades, life was thought to be pretty simple. A bacterium was considered to be a cell membrane surrounding a small amount of water and a nucleus. Multi-celled organisms were considered more or less to be a gathering of single-celled organisms that had learned to cooperate. Thus the creation of life was thought to be pretty simple as well. From the 1950s through the 1970s, a prevailing theory about the very beginnings of life was called the "primordial soup" model. It was thought that about 380 million years ago there existed pools of water with small organic molecules floating about. Such pools do not create life by themselves, so it was proposed that a bolt of lightning struck a pool of this primordial soup, which triggered a set of organic reactions necessary to form larger organic molecules. Once begun, these organics initiated a cascade of further reactions that formed all the molecules needed for life. According to this theory, these molecules then all came together to spontaneously create life.

Given that hypothesis, for decades scientists combined varieties of organic molecules (soups) and applying energy in the form of electric sparks (lightning) or heat, trying to create life. After all, life is found all over the earth, from the deepest oceans to the highest mountains, from frozen tundra to the edges of volcanos. Life is so widespread, how hard could it be to create it? Obviously, there is a Nobel Prize waiting for the first successful researcher to accomplish this feat. However, so far, no one has been successful. This is not a surprise.

First of all, life is hard to define. Is the simplest form of life a single-cell plant, like a fungus or algae? Is the simplest life form microbiological, such as simple bacteria? Or is it a virus or a prion? The debate around this topic is endless. Most agree, however, on at least two requirements. First, a living organism had to have the basic processes of life, such as energy (food) intake, digestion to obtain the energy in that food, and waste elimination. Second, the organism has to be self-replicating. No living thing has figured out how to live forever. So whatever organism can be credited with being the first life on Earth, it had to be able to create new copies of itself. By definition, life must continue to live.

But life is not simple; it is complex. The complexity of single cell biology has taken centuries of work to uncover, and we are not yet done. The complexity of multicellular organisms is even more confusing. In this chapter, I would like to review a couple of the components of life that illustrate this complexity. Once again we must decide if we attribute the existence of these components and the life they allow to incredible luck or to a master Creator, Biochemist, and God.

PROTEINS

Our bodies themselves and every single bodily function require proteins. Proteins make up over half of the dry matter in our bodies. Much of this protein, such as collagen, is structural in nature. These proteins give both strength and flexibility to skin, bones, muscle, and connective tissues. But the majority of the different types of proteins in the body are active molecules that actually drive the processes of life. Enzymes digest our food, hemoglobin transports oxygen in our blood stream, and antibodies fight disease and infection. Muscles move your body and the heart pumps your blood. Hormones are the messengers for cell-to-cell communication and regulate most of your bodily functions. The bacteria in your colon depend on proteins to determine which extracellular molecules are allowed to enter the cell and which are not. Proteins break down the cell's food for energy and then escort waste products out of the cell. It is certain that any life as we know it needs proteins.

Proteins, in comparison to the other components of our body, are very complex. Lipids, for example, are simply long strings of fatty acids. Polysaccharides are long strings of a few different sugars. But these latter two structures are not complex enough to carry information or perform specific functions for the cell or body. Proteins have their complex structure to allow them to be the body's workhorses. They are produced in cells from DNA blueprints using combinations of 20 different amino acids. Just like our alphabet of 26 letters is used to write a book, these 20 amino acids are used to create proteins. But just like a good story cannot have many misspelled words, a functioning protein cannot have many misplaced amino acids. These amino acids must come together to give each protein both its three-dimensional structure and the molecular bonding capabilities it requires to do its job.

Hemoglobin, a protein that must hold an iron atom in place to transport oxygen from the blood to our body tissues, needs all of its 146 amino acids to accurately position the iron to accomplish its task. Amylase, the enzyme in our saliva and stomach tasked with breaking down the starch in our food, has 496 amino acids. The structural protein collagen needs its 1,055 amino acids to be correctly positioned to allow it to interact with other collagen chains to provide the strength of bone and elasticity of skin and muscle.[1] The largest known protein of the human body is titin, a protein important for muscle contraction, which weighs in at an impressive ~30,000 amino acids. That number is an approximation since titin can be different, depending on the muscle in which it resides. The titin found in skeletal muscle will have a sequence of amino acids that optimize it to meet the requirements of skeletal muscle; the titin found in cardiac muscle is optimized for cardiac functions.[2]

THE MATH OF MAKING PROTEINS

What is the probability of making a relatively small protein, say a starch-digesting amylase of just 200 amino acids, from a random pool of all of the amino acids? First let's say we would need the amino acid glycine to take the end spot. Since there are 20 amino acids, the chances of this happening are one chance in twenty (1/20). Then let's assume we need tryptophan to take the second position; the chances of this happening are also 1/20. But, if you remember your high school math, the chance of both glycine and tryptophan being in their correct positions is 1/20 *multiplied by* 1/20, or 1/400. This exercise in probability continues. Let's say the third amino acid in the chain must be leucine, but the odds of the glycine—tryptophan—leucine chain forming are now 1/8000. We now must add on another 197 amino acids. To calculate the chance of the full protein being made in the proper sequence is 20 to the power of 200 (20^{200}) or 1 chance in 10^{260}. Before the biologists can object to my math, let me add a disclaimer that there are some locations in proteins that may be filled by one of several amino acids. Thus, let's round down our chance of a successful, randomly-constructed protein of 200 amino acids to 1 chance in an octogintillion. The odds of winning a recent large Powerball jackpot were reported as 1 in 292.2 million. Thus you have a better chance of winning Powerball lotteries every year for 40 years than you would of randomly building a 200 amino acid protein.

But we are not done with our probability exercise. A cell needs more than one protein to survive. To make a second protein of the same chain length, let's say of a protein-digesting protease this time, would have the same probability of success as our amylase. The odds of making both the amylase and the protease would be 1 chance in 10^{260} *times* 1 chance in 10^{260}, or 1 chance in 10^{520}. With such odds, you can either believe we are very, very lucky or you can believe protein making is a preprogrammed process, written very long ago by a divine Creator.

DNA

So, in the world of biology, proteins are amazing. The only biological molecule more amazing is DNA, also known as deoxyribonucleic acid. DNA is the blueprint to make every protein in your body. Each cell in our body is programmed to read those blueprints and construct the proteins that make up the cell. DNA was first identified in 1869 by Swiss chemist Friedrich Miescher. For decades, it was considered an unimportant material and proteins were given the credit for passing on family traits. Then, in 1944, it was shown by a group of microbiologists that it was actually DNA that transferred characteristics from one generation to the next.

To determine how DNA worked, scientists first had to determine its structure. In 1953, James Watson and Francis Crick determined that DNA was constructed as a double helix. To understand a double helix, picture in your mind a very long spiral staircase. The inside and outside supports are made up of long molecules of phosphates and sugars and are merely structural in purpose. The "stairs" between the supports are where the genetic information is stored. Each stair is made up of deoxyribose, phosphate, and two of four "bases"—cytosine (C), thymine (T), adenine (A), or guanine (G). The two bases connect in the middle of the stair. The "C" base is always attached to a "G" base, while a "T" base is always attached to an "A" base. Each linkage of the two bases is called a base pair.

When the cell needs to build a protein, the DNA temporarily breaks a number of "steps" (or base pairs) right down the middle. As the DNA unzips itself, one half of the zipper uses components in the cell to build a new segment. Since a "G" base can only attach to a "C" base and a "T" base will only connect to an "A," it is actually hard for a mistake to be made. This newly constructed segment, a single strand looking like a ladder split down the middle, is called messenger RNA, or mRNA for short. The mRNA makes its way out of the nucleus and into the ribosome where the mRNA is read and the new proteins are constructed. Every three rungs of the split ladder specify one particular amino acid. For example, the series of three bases GAA direct the cell to add the amino acid glutamic acid to the protein under construction. The next set of three bases selects the next amino acid that will be added to the protein chain. Gradually, as the mRNA blueprint is followed, the protein grows longer until it is completed and sent off on its mission.

Within any particular organism, there can be tens of thousands of distinct mRNAs doing their work, each directing the construction of its own distinct protein. From those mRNA molecules, proteins are made very quickly. Ribosomes can join about 200 amino acids per minute and, in a mammalian cell, there can be several million ribosomes. So every second thousands of proteins can be manufactured by a single cell.[1]

When a cell is going to divide, it needs to replicate its DNA, so the copy can be sent off in the new cell. This replication process is very similar to the construction of mRNA. The DNA completely unzips itself and each half makes a new DNA molecule from the building blocks at hand. The DNA reproduction requires a number of proteins to accomplish its task. Proteases separate the double helix and binding proteins stabilize the single strand structure. Polymerases assemble the new DNA and proofread it, ejecting any mismatched nucleotides that have been added to the chain. Finally, ligases add the final bonds to the newly formed DNA.

There is one more reason for DNA to replicate itself. To pass your genes on to your sons and daughters, very specialized cells in your body use the same DNA duplication. The copy of your DNA is then built into a sperm or an egg and sent forth as part of your reproductive biology. When the time is right, a strand of DNA from the sperm and one from the egg will come together. This unique DNA will then start to make the proteins that will make other proteins that will, after about nine months, make a complete human being. It is an amazing process. So you have heard the old conundrum of "What came first, the chicken or the egg?" Each is needed to make the other. Here is a similar mystery that has baffled biologists. If proteins are needed to make DNA and DNA is needed to make proteins, which came first?

THE COMPLEXITY OF DNA

We could run another mathematical exercise to determine the probability of making DNA randomly. But the chances would be outrageously slim. Each of you has two genomes of 3 billion base pairs each, one from your mother and one from your father. Transcription errors occur at a rate of only one error in every 100 million base pairs. Thus we each have about 60 new mutations in our genetics that were not part of our parents. This allows us some room for uniqueness, though there is a slim chance that those mutations can also cause serious dysfunctions. These mutations are however, a critical part of evolution. If a mutation turns out to be an improvement in the ability of the mutated plant or animal to survive or reproduce, that mutation will be passed on to future generations. A small improvement in the chance to survive and reproduce is magnified in those descendent generations and the mutation can eventually become an established trait in some of the species. So DNA strikes a most unlikely balance. First, it has the ability to almost flawlessly pass genetics from parent to child. But the "almost" is critically important too. Generally, the mutations that arise from transcription mistakes are detrimental to the individual—often they die because of them. But sometimes the mutation is beneficial and the individual thrives, eventually changing the whole species.

JUST NOT ENOUGH TIME

When presented with these, let's face it, impossible odds, atheists argued that given billions of years even something as wildly improbable as randomly-constructed proteins could happen. In 1954, George Wald, a Harvard University biochemist and Nobel Laureate wrote, "Time is in fact the hero of the plot. The time with which we have to deal is of the order of two billion years. What we regard as impossible on the basis of human experience is meaningless here. Given so much time, the 'impossible' becomes possible, the possible probable, and the probable virtually certain. One has only to wait: time itself performs the miracles."[3]

It turns out that Dr. Wald was wrong. Twenty-five years later, *Scientific American* retracted the article, stating that Wald was wrong and "that merely to create a single bacterium would require more time than the universe might ever see if chance combinations of its molecules were the only driving force." Five years after that, in 1984, Dr. Wald admitted there is a driving force behind evolution, stating, "It is mind that has composed a physical universe that breeds life and so eventually evolves creatures that know and create: science-, art-, and technology-making animals."[4] Simon Conway Morris, a paleobiologist at Cambridge stated, "The number of potential 'blind alleys' is so enormous that in principle all the time since the beginning of the universe would be insufficient to find the one in a trillion trillion solutions that actually work."[5]

The point to all this discussion so far is that the Big Bang, the creation of Earth, the beginnings of life, and the evolution of plants, animals, and humans could not have been random or undirected. These three events were far too complicated for them to have occurred by lucky chance. They say that nothing is impossible, but this really is impossible. As illustrated by the examples of flipping coins or rolling dice, if we don't accept one-in-a-billion-chance/random luck explanations, then we have to look for a behind-the-scenes Creator who was the mastermind behind the whole creation event. Thus we must accept the fact that creation was directed by God.

We don't understand how such a thing was done. How much work did God have to do? Was He overseeing the Creation on a continuous basis, or was He able to stop by the Earth every million years or so to check on progress? Though I personally believe the latter explanation is closer to reality, we don't know, nor do we really have to know. Much of the work was obviously programmed into DNA since, through mutation, DNA can try out different combinations. By changes in its sequencing, DNA can produce uniquely different proteins to see if they are more efficient or powerful. Life, the Earth, and the universe are all very complex, and the Creation had to weave them together. Whether you look at it from a scientific, artistic, or religious point of view, the Creation was an amazing piece of work.

It is probable that there are going to be critics of this concept from both those who believe in evolution without God (atheists) and those who believe in creation without evolution (pure creationists). The belief being presented is a middle ground between these two extremes. The faithful followers of God believe that God can hear the prayers of millions of His children at the same time. Is the possibility that He could have directed evolution while attending to other responsibilities and developing other worlds all that strange?

NOTES

1. Bill Bryson, *A Short History of Nearly Everything* (New York: Broadway Books: 2003), 288, 378.
2. "Titin," Protopedia. http://proteopedia.org/wiki/index.php/Titin.
3. George Wald, *The Origin of Life*, vol. 191 of *Scientific American* (August 1954), 44–53.
4. Gerald L. Schroeder, *God According to God* (New York: Harper One, 2009), 49.
5. Ibid., 47.

THE SIX DAYS
OF GENESIS

n the LDS Church, we have three scriptural accounts of the Creation: Genesis chapters 1–2, Moses chapters 2–3, and Abraham chapters 4–5. Two of these scriptures originated from the same original account written by Moses. Over the centuries, we believe changes, mistranslations, or typos have made their way into the Genesis account. Though it seems apparent that Abraham had the same vision that Moses would receive years later, Abraham emphasized different aspects of the revelation than Moses. Thus, there are some differences, mostly minor, found among the three accounts. Though a verse-by-verse comparison will not be attempted here, there are some insights that can be gained from the different accounts.

Science provides us yet a fourth account of the Creation. There have been dozens of books written comparing the Genesis account of the Creation with that of science. Since the intent of this book is to show that a mental testimony of God can be strengthened by observations of nature and the findings of science, a review of the first six creation periods of Genesis may be in order.

Moses and Abraham were not college-educated men. Neither was John the Revelator, nor Lehi, nor Joseph Smith. The revelations that these men received and reported had to be interpreted within the context of their understanding. Probably the best example of a prophet struggling to explain what he had seen in vision may be found in the book of Revelation. The apostle John tries to explain, through description and symbolism, his vision of the Apocalypse. But Moses and Abraham had their own challenges. They saw a vision that included astronomy, chemistry, microbiology, plant biology, animal biology and the creation of man. Both reported what they had seen as accurately as possible, based on what they understood of those fields at the time. Both of these men were mighty prophets of God, but they were not scientists.

So, today, with the sciences' descriptions of the Creation in hand, we can read Moses's and Abraham's accounts of their visions and consider what they might have actually meant. As we find consistencies, the scientific account of creation can actually become another testimony that the scriptural accounts are true. We can also develop better insight into what these scriptures may be describing. So, taking each "day" of the Creation, I would like to propose interpretations for what Moses and Abraham saw in their visions.

DAY ONE

According to Genesis, on the first day of Creation,

> And God said, Let there be light: and there was light.
> And God saw the light, that it was good: and God divided the light from the darkness.
> And God called the light Day, and the darkness he called Night. (Genesis 1:3–5)

However, jumping ahead a bit in the Creation story, on the *fourth* day, we learn that,

> And God made two great lights; the greater light to rule the day, and the lesser light to rule the night: he made the stars also.
> And God set them in the firmament of the heaven to give light upon the earth. (Genesis 1:16–17)

If God actually created sunlight on the first day, why did He have to create it again on the fourth day? The only sources of light the earth has had from its beginning comes from the sun, or from the stars, or the reflected sunlight on the moon. What light did He actually create on Day One? Are the scriptures just being redundant or are we are missing something here?

There is an explanation that both removes the redundancy and allows us to follow the order of our scientific account of the Creation. As stated earlier, the Big Bang was the first step in the Creation. Nothing existed before the Big Bang—no space, no light, no matter, no time. The Big Bang was the most powerful explosion of energy in the history of the universe. Let us consider a moment—if Moses had seen the Big Bang in a revelatory vision of the beginnings of the universe, how would he have described it? Moses saw a vision of the Creation of the world and he wrote down what he saw, much like Lehi, Nephi, Isaiah, Daniel, Peter, John the Revelator, and other prophets.

At the very beginnings of his vision, before the Big Bang, Moses would have seen a perfect darkness, since no light existed. "And the earth was without form, and void; and darkness was upon the face of the deep" (Genesis 1:2). A void is a completely empty space. The "deep" can be pictured as an ocean, but it also means a vast extent of space or time. With these two definitions in mind, Moses can be given credit for a good description of space before the Big Bang. Then Moses would have seen an enormous explosion of light and matter that would have filled the universe. Moses, as almost anyone would have done, concluded that he had just witnessed the creation of all light.

Moses then goes on to write, "And God saw the light, that it was good: and God divided the light from the darkness." In a fast-forwarded vision of the next ten billion years after the Big Bang, this is exactly what Moses would have seen. Through gravity's pull, galaxies would have been created and, within those galaxies, millions of suns would have formed. There would have been patches of intense light at the centers of these galaxies. But between those suns and galaxies would have been light-years of dark space. Moses would have seen millions of divisions of light from darkness. Again, his words seem a logical way to describe such a breathtaking scene.

On first reading, we might consider the phrase in Genesis 1:4 "and God divided the light from the darkness" to mean the separation of day and night, since in Genesis 1:5 "God called the light Day, and the darkness he called Night." But, again, the creation task of separating day and night occurs on Day Four (Genesis 1:18) where God set the sun and the moon in the firmament "to rule over the day and over the night, and to divide the light from the darkness." Though similar in wording, these two phrases are different in meaning. In summary, on the first day, about 14 billion years ago, God brought about the Big Bang. Over the next ten billion years, light separated from darkness as millions of suns and galaxies separated themselves from the blackness of space. This was the first creation event and it took a very long time. Moses described it with poetry that, in just a few words, communicates the beauty of it, if not the details.

MATTER UNORGANIZED

Still during the first creative period called Day One, but about 8 billion years ago, a galaxy now called the Milky Way was formed. Within that galaxy, in our neighborhood of space, there was a large interstellar cloud made of hydrogen, helium, and some heavier elements made in earlier suns. Over millions of years, this nebula gradually collapsed into what is now our solar system. This particular time in the history of the solar system is of particular note to LDS Church members. At some point in that time period, the Creator Jesus Christ looked down upon our future home and announced, "We will go down, for there is space there, and we will take of these materials, and we will make an earth whereon these may dwell" (Abraham 3:24). Just a few verses later, the Gods "organized and formed the heavens and the earth" (Abraham 4:1).

DAY TWO

> And God said, Let there be a firmament in the midst of the waters, and let it divide the waters from the waters.
>
> And God made the firmament, and divided the waters which were under the firmament from the waters which were above the firmament: and it was so.
>
> And God called the firmament Heaven. And the evening and the morning were the second day. (Genesis 1:6–8)

In the account of the book of Abraham, the word "firmament" is replaced with the word "expanse." In Moses's day, the Israelites shared the belief that the sky was a solid dome with the sun, moon, and stars embedded in it. This dome was called the firmament. Bible critics have made much ado about how ridiculous the notion was. A firmament is what early translators pictured from the description given, but the word "expanse" is actually more descriptive and probably a better translation. In any case, what was Moses trying to describe?

During its formative years about 4.5 billion years ago, the earth was not a gentle place to be. Due to the leftover energy dispelled with its gravitational collapse, the earth was very hot. Asteroids pummeled the planet regularly as the earth cleared its orbit of the debris from the nebula collapse. There was, of course, no atmosphere. But, in the course of time, an atmosphere was gradually formed by outgassing both of gases trapped in the interior of the Earth (a process which still goes on today in volcanoes) and of gases created by reactions occurring in the magma and rocks. But this was not an atmosphere that we could breathe. It contained little oxygen and quite a few gases that would have been poisonous to us, such as hydrogen sulfide (the rotten-egg-smelling gas you can smell quite easily from the pools and geysers at Yellowstone Park). Plants were not going to grow in such a hostile environment either.

Over time, the earth cooled. But for the creation of life to continue, a breathable atmosphere consisting mostly of nitrogen and oxygen was needed. It was a necessary, monumental task—and it was carried out during Day Two. In reading the words, "And the Gods ordered the expanse," it is not hard to picture our atmosphere. The atmosphere is, of course, invisible, so Moses may have viewed the atmosphere as a way to "separate the waters" and this was probably the best way he could explain it. Less than 0.001% of all of the water on Earth is actually in the atmosphere.[1] But that water was vitally important as it becomes the rains and snow that would keep the earth watered. Without it, the whole earth would be a desert. Moses may have seen the beneficial effects of an atmosphere that would allow rain and described it in the best way he could.

The terms "firmament" and "expanse" are open for interpretation. In Abraham 4:8 the expanse is called Heaven, which brings up one visual image. In Abraham 4:20, the Gods prepared the waters to bring forth the fowl "that they may fly above the earth in the open expanse of heaven." This statement indicates the expanse is the sky or the atmosphere, which better fits our interpretation of the events of Day Two.

We believe that God makes use of natural means to bring about his will. So, how did He create an atmosphere? About 3.5 billion years ago, single-celled organisms (which would evolve into our present-day bacteria) appeared in the oceans. This event was monumental since bacteria were the first organisms that could be termed "life." None of the scriptural creation accounts document the beginnings of life in the form of microscopic organisms. If he had seen that step in his revelatory vision, Moses would have had a really tough time explaining what he saw, since microscopes would not be invented for thousands of years. But science tells us that microorganisms arrived long before any other form of life.

These first single-celled organisms were tough little guys. They could survive in the poisonous atmosphere of the time. They used the carbon dioxide and noxious elements of our early world to survive and grow. Then, about 3 billion years ago, cyanobacteria evolved with improved photosynthetic abilities. Photosynthesis both consumes carbon dioxide and produces oxygen, which is exactly what our world needed for life to evolve. For millions of years, all of the oxygen that was released by these cyanobacteria was soaked up by iron and organic matter dissolved in the oceans, holding the global oxygen levels at about 3%. About 2.4 billion years ago, the earth had absorbed all the oxygen it could hold, and oxygen started to build up in the atmosphere. Over the next two million years, the earth experienced its Great Oxygenation Event and oxygen levels soared. Gradually, the percentage of oxygen in the atmosphere stabilized to the 21% level that we enjoy today.

Meanwhile, ammonia, which was very plentiful in early Earth's atmosphere, was being decomposed by sunlight, oxygen, and certain bacteria into the nitrogen that now makes up 78% of our atmosphere. Our atmosphere had been formed and water existed both in that atmosphere and on the surface of the earth below. The tasks of Day Two were complete.

DAY THREE

Day Three brings about two events. First, dry land is separated from the seas and secondly, grass, herbs, and trees make their appearance. From the Genesis account,

> And God said, Let the waters under the heaven be gathered together unto one place, and let the dry land appear: and it was so.
>
> And God called the dry land Earth; and the gathering together of the waters called he Seas: and God saw that it was good.
>
> And God said, Let the earth bring forth grass, the herb yielding seed, and the fruit tree yielding fruit after his kind, whose seed is in itself, upon the earth: and it was so.
>
> And the earth brought forth grass, and herb yielding seed after his kind, and the tree yielding fruit, whose seed was in itself, after his kind: and God saw that it was good. (Genesis 1:9–12)

LET THE DRY LAND APPEAR

Initially Earth's surface was mostly molten rock that gradually cooled to form a stable rocky crust. Since it had been a molten liquid and liquids spread out evenly on a surface, the earth had little topography. There were no significant mountains, no valleys, and no deep oceans. Naturally, the water on top of the earth was also spread out evenly on its surface. So, about 3 billion years ago, dry land was very hard to find on our planet, as water covered over 95% of the surface. Unless Earth was to remain a water world, we needed more dry land.

Over time, cooler parts of Earth's crust sunk down under the warmer upper mantle. Eventually the crust would heal itself, but these sunken land masses stayed intact and became what are now called tectonic plates. These plates essentially float on the hot magma mantle underneath Earth's crust upon which we stand. Since that magma constantly recirculates, the plates move, sometimes dragging entire continents along with them. Over the millennia, when these plates collided, the rocks and dirt of the crust had to go somewhere. Some of the crust folded up to form massive mountain ranges and lands that rose above sea level. As that happened, dry land literally appeared, rising above the ocean surface. Vast valleys and canyons were also created and, once filled with run-off water, these became our oceans, seas, and lakes.

In this way, the land masses that formed the continents started to emerge from our vast but shallow ocean. As the dry lands continued to appear, there is convincing evidence that they moved around quite a bit in a process called continental drift. The continents have not always been in the same position they are today (and they are still moving, albeit slowly). The first supercontinent, called Ur, emerged about three billion years ago. It grew, merged with other land masses, broke apart, and rearranged itself again to form continents called Arctica, Baltica, and Atlantica. About one billion years ago the supercontinent of Rodinia was formed, then Panotia. Finally, about 300 million years ago, the most recent and well-known supercontinent Pangea was formed. When it broke up about 175 million years ago, the pieces spread apart to eventually take their places as the continents we recognize today.[2] At the latest count, about 28% of Earth's surface is above sea level. The dry land had appeared.

THE PLANTS

The first life to appear on the earth was the single-celled predecessors of the cyanobacteria just mentioned. These small and simple organisms, really little more than an "algae scum," were capable of photosynthesis but not of living outside of water. This situation lasted for about two billion years. It is very unlikely that algae is what the Creator meant when he commanded the earth to "bring forth grass, the herb yielding seed, and the fruit tree yielding fruit." The earth was getting ready to bring forth plants, but was not quite ready to do so.

Evidence for the appearance of the first spore-forming land plants (such as the mosses) occurred around 460 million years ago. But they were limited to moist environments and could not spread out to dry land. In order to photosynthesize, plants must absorb CO_2 from the atmosphere. However, this respiration comes at a price since as plants absorb CO_2, water inside the plant evaporates. Water is, of course, critical to plants, so they needed to constantly replace it. Plant life had to evolve internal vascular systems that could transport water from the moist soil to all parts of the plants, before they could make their move onto land.

Ferns, the first plants to develop this capability, appear in the fossil record about 360 million years ago and initiated the extensive land colonization by plants. But they were still very limited in the heights they could attain, because a vine could only grow so far before it collapsed under its own weight. Taller plants had an advantage over their competitors in that their top leaves could gather more sunlight for photosynthesis. But for trees to develop, early plants had to evolve to grow strong woody tissue in their trunks and branches to provide structural support for taller growth. Once plants had developed this capability, the trees that would provide man with both wood and fruit could start their growth. The earliest trees were conifers (or gymnosperms) which are cone-bearing trees such as pines, spruce, fir, and junipers. Conifers appeared in the fossil record date about 300 million years ago and were the dominant land plants by within 50 million years.

Returning now to Genesis, it is significant to consider the specific plants that the Lord used as examples of all the plants to come forth. "Let the earth bring forth grass, the herb yielding seed, and the fruit tree yielding fruit after his kind, whose seed is in itself" (Genesis 1:11). Grass, herbs that yield seed, and fruit trees yielding fruit with seeds are all examples of the flowering plants, also known as angiosperms.

It would appear that God gave the command for the flowering plants to come forth about 125 million years ago, because that is when they started to appear. They appeared in a big way too. Today, angiosperms make up about 80 percent of all the green plants now living.[3] Flowering plants gradually gained dominance in the plant kingdom for two reasons. First, beetles, bees, butterflies, and other insects had multiplied to become very efficient nectar-collecting pollinators of all those flowers. Secondly, once fertilized, a flowering plant produces fruit. Animals of the time (both dinosaurs and early mammals) consumed those fruits and scattered the seeds far and wide.[4] The flowering plants evolved to take advantage of the local wildlife to scatter its seeds to all parts of the world.

The last major group of plants to evolve was the grasses, whose origin can be dated by the appearance of grass pollen in the fossil record about 60 million years ago. Due to their drought tolerance and capacity to thrive in dry, open habitats, grasses became a major player in the plant family around 30 million years ago. Grasses cover vast regions in the prairies of North America, the savannas of Africa, and the grasslands of South America.[5] One may still wonder why grasses got first billing in the command for the earth to bring forth plants, but since grasses include rice, wheat, oats, and maize, extremely important sources of our food intake, one should be able to better appreciate their importance.

THE OVERLAP OF CREATIVE PERIODS

The Big Bang of Day One occurred about 14 billion years ago and, it could be argued, continues to this day. The build-up of our atmosphere during Day Two lasted between 3 billion to 2 billion years ago. Day Three first saw the emergence of dry land, which started at the same time, 3 billion years ago to about 60 million years ago, when continental drift placed the continents in their present positions. But Day Three also included the emergence of plants on that dry land, which occurred from 360 million years ago to 30 million years ago.

Because the Genesis account is so explicit and repetitive regarding the sequence of creation periods, it is easy to think of each creation period as being in consecutive order and that each period ended before the next began. But the fossil record indicates there was a great deal of overlap between essentially all of the six creation periods. As Bruce R. McConkie taught, a day, as used in the Creation accounts "is a specified time period; it is an age, an eon, a division of eternity; it is the time between two identifiable events. And each day, of whatever length, has the duration needed for its purposes."[6] Though it may appear superficially that each creative period is consecutive, the scriptures never state that this is the case. Read in this light, there is less and less discrepancy between the Genesis account and the fossil record.

DAY FOUR

The understanding that the six creative periods did not have to be consecutive and could overlap helps a great deal in understanding Day Four.
In Day Three, the earth is instructed to bring forth plants. But how are
plants supposed to survive with no sun? Simply put, they cannot. The
sun would have had to be in place before the earth could possibly bring
forth living plants. The sun is about 4.5 billion years old, close to the
same age as the earth. Thus, in Day Four, God reveals the two great
lights set in the firmament of heaven.

> And God said, Let there be lights in the firmament of the heaven
> to divide the day from the night; and let them be for signs, and for
> seasons, and for days, and years:
> And let them be for lights in the firmament of the heaven to give
> light upon the earth: and it was so.
> And God made two great lights; the greater light to rule the day,
> and the lesser light to rule the night: he made the stars also.
> And God set them in the firmament of the heaven to give light
> upon the earth,
> And to rule over the day and over the night, and to divide
> the light from the darkness: and God saw that it was good.
> (Genesis 1:14–18)

So, Day Four could have been a description of the formation of
our solar system. But, this hardly makes sense since the sun had to
be in place before Day Two (for even bacteria cannot survive without
the sun) and certainly before Day Three when the plants were commanded to grow. But there is another possible way to interpret Day
Four. During the time the earth was cooling, any water on the ground
evaporated, rose into the atmosphere, cooled, and fell as rain. This
happened everywhere on the earth for millennia. As the atmosphere
was being created, as the dry land appeared, and as the plants were
just starting to grow, it probably rained all the time. Thus the sun and
the moon were not placed in the heavens on Day Four. But the clouds
finally dissipated and the light of the sun and the moon were allowed to
appear. You can find this interpretation in both LDS and Jewish teachings. For example, in the temple narrative describing this event, God's
commandment was specifically to "cause the lights in the firmament

to appear." This wording implies that the lights had been there before, but now were caused to appear. Bruce R. McConkie stated about the fourth day that "during this period the sun, moon and stars assumed the relationship to the earth that now is theirs. At least the light of each of them began to shine through the lifting hazes that enshrouded the newly created earth."[6] In discussing this same creation event, Gerald L. Schroeder, a prominent Jewish scholar and author stated, "But the sun is mentioned only on day four (though the ancient commentaries tell us that the sun was there earlier, but only became visible in the sky on the fourth day)."[7]

DAY FIVE

And God said, Let the waters bring forth abundantly the moving creature that hath life, and fowl that may fly above the earth in the open firmament of heaven.

And God created great whales, and every living creature that moveth, which the waters brought forth abundantly, after their kind, and every winged fowl after his kind: and God saw that it was good.

And God blessed them, saying, Be fruitful, and multiply, and fill the waters in the seas, and let fowl multiply in the earth. (Genesis 1:20–22)

It is especially significant that the scriptures state that God did not personally create marine life or the birds. He delegated the task and commanded the waters to do it. While God set the beginnings of life in motion, the *waters* were to actually bring forth the creatures that have life. From his wording, it seems apparent that Moses saw life emerge from the waters. If you were to see a very fast-forwarded history of the earth, how would marine evolution have looked? Moses may have seen the arrival of small fishes, shrimp, and shellfish. He would have seen this small marine life gradually become larger and more varied. It is probable that Moses did not understand the science of evolutionary marine biology that was laid out for him in vision. To him, it would have appeared that the waters had simply brought "forth abundantly the moving creature that hath life." But in doing so, Moses still recognized that the waters had been commanded to do this task.

It is also very significant to note that the scriptures state that the waters were to bring forth abundantly *the moving creature that hath life*, and fowl *that* may fly above the earth . . ." That is an all-inclusive list. What animal life would be excluded from that description? By definition, animals are all moving creatures, whether that movement is by tentacles, fins, wings, or legs. It seems a distinct possibility that Moses was recognizing that all animal life started in the oceans, a conclusion with which science agrees. It should be noted that "And God created great whales" may have been an overly-limiting translation. Newer translations of the Bible all use phrases such as "large sea creatures" and "great sea monsters." Moses could have seen 16-foot Jurassic ichthyosaurs and then 40-foot pliosaurs and plesiosaurs, the most fearsome carnivores of the marine dinosaurs.[8] "Great sea monsters" would have been an apt description of them. But then again, Moses may have seen 90-foot blue whales in his revelation as well. In either case, the creatures were impressive enough to merit his special recognition in Genesis 1:21.

Day Six—The Morning

Like Day Three, Day Six includes two major events in the creative process. First, land animals are told to come forth from the ground and then, man is created.

> And God said, Let the earth bring forth the living creature after his kind, cattle, and creeping thing, and beast of the earth after his kind: and it was so.
> And God made the beast of the earth after his kind, and cattle after their kind, and every thing that creepeth upon the earth after his kind: and God saw that it was good. (Genesis 1:24–25)

The Animals

Evolutionary biologists generally all agree that life started in the oceans. Some of the smaller creatures of the ocean moved to the coastal regions, where the tides exposed these hardy animals to dry land for certain parts of the day. Eventually these animals evolved and developed the lungs needed to survive on dry land. Once on land, a whole new set of living creatures emerged. First came the amphibians and reptiles, which grew and then grew some more. From 225 million years ago to 65 million years ago, dinosaurs ruled the earth. With the extinction of the dinosaurs, small mammals were then able to continue their evolution and grow larger themselves. Mammals, the class of animals to which we belong, have ruled the world ever since.

Moses would also have seen this series of events in his vision. It must have been a dizzying experience for him to see the number and variety of land animals that came forth. Just as it had appeared to him that the waters had brought forth marine life, birds and every moving creature, it would now have appeared that the earth brought forth its own abundance of life. It is interesting to note that Moses again recognized that the Lord had delegated the task of bringing forth the land animals to the earth. He didn't do it Himself.

DID GOD OR EVOLUTION DO MOST OF THE CREATION WORK?

Genesis 1:25 is a great segue into the next point, when it states, "And God made the beast of the earth after his kind, and cattle after their kind, and every thing that creepeth upon the earth after his kind: and God saw that it was good." Now that we are toward the end of the Creation story, we might ask, "Did God or evolution do most of the work?" How much of the Creation was wrought personally by God and how much was accomplished by evolution?

Each person who believes in God and evolution will have their own opinion on this matter, but let's start at one extreme and work our way back. Let's say that God actually had to engineer each species of plant, insect, and animal on the earth. Just in the realm of insects, the task would be huge as well as tedious. Not counting the insects that have gone extinct, about 1,000,000 different species of bugs have been identified and given a taxonomic description. There are about 350,000 species of beetles and about 150,000 species of flies. These numbers only include the species that have been catalogued of course. It is estimated that there are actually 4,000,000–6,000,000 species of insects.[9] In your perception of God's job, do you picture that He had to select and engineer the differences in millions of species of insects, fishes, reptiles, and mammals? Is it God's job to be a species designer, picking out the mandibles, leg shapes, and coloring of every one of the 350,000 species of beetles? Isn't it easier to imagine that evolution, with its ability to optimize species for their specific environment, created this diversity?

I wouldn't wish such the job of bug designer on anyone, even if he had millions of years to accomplish it. So it is much easier for me to believe that God has a tool, whether you call it evolution or DNA, which creates these millions of species automatically, with little oversight. On the other extreme, it is hard for me to believe that random variations of DNA would allow all species of plants and animals to blindly, yet adeptly, stumble ahead to flourish in their environment. There had to be a guiding force to help it along. DNA can do a lot, but I believe we are missing the whole picture. Thus I believe in both God the Creator and the tool of evolution. Exactly how the Creator used that tool is still an unknown.

MASS EXTINCTIONS

It is interesting to consider the process and timeframe that God used to create the world. As queried in earlier chapters, did God have to oversee the Creation on a day-to-day basis or was He able to stop by the earth every million years or so to check on its progress? However, there is some evidence that the Creation was often left to proceed on its own since it took a number of detours along the way. Multiple mass extinctions are scattered throughout the fossil record. These mass extinctions caused the loss of an enormous number of plant and animal species from the earth.

About twenty global mass extinctions have been identified in the history of our world.[10] The oldest of these extinctions is called the Ordovician-Silurian extinction, which occurred 444 million years ago. This was before life had established itself on land, so the approximately 85% loss of species all occurred in the ocean. Next came the Late Devonian extinction, which happened about 364 million years ago. We lost about half of Earth's animals and plants to that event. The worst loss of plant, animal, and marine life was called the Permian-Triassic extinction, which occurred about 250 million years ago and caused the loss of about 75% of all species present on the earth at the time. The Late Triassic (225 million years ago) and the Triassic-Jurassic extinctions (208 million years ago) each extinguished about half of the world's species. This last event signaled the beginning of the Age of Dinosaurs, which lasted for about 160 million years. But then the most well-known mass extinction, the Cretaceous-Tertiary (also called the K-T extinction), occurred 66 million years ago. This extinction toppled the dinosaurs from their throne by killing off all but for a very few of the smallest dinosaur species.[10]

We do not know for certain what global tragedies caused these extinctions. Global ice ages, possibly catalyzed by volcanic eruptions (that put enough ash and sulfur into the upper atmosphere to significantly block sunlight), are blamed for many of them. It is thought that the dinosaur-ending K-T extinction was initiated by a meteorite that struck near the Gulf of Mexico and possibly started its own global ice age. In any case, it took millions of years for the earth to recover from each extinction as completely new species of plants and animals had to evolve and repopulate the land and sea. If God had been personally designing, building, and placing all of these species on Earth to prepare it for mankind, why did He allow so many mass extinctions to set His work back for millions of years? It doesn't seem to make any sense. However, if evolution was acting as a programmed biological process doing its job, it would continue to evolve new species to fill in the biological niches in every part of the world. Such set-backs would simply be a part of the evolution story and not global tragedies engineered by God to interrupt and delay His work. Whatever global tragedy caused each extinction, evolution would continue in its function of expanding the variety and survivability of life.

NOTES

1. USGS Website: https://www.usgs.gov/
2. Ted Nield, *Supercontinent: Ten Billion Years in the Life of Our Planet* (Harvard University Press, 2007).

3. "When Dinosaurs Ruled," National Geographic Special Edition (Feb 2016).
4. Stephen Jay Gould, *The Book of Life* (New York: W. W. Norton, 1993), 152–157.
5. Elizabeth Kellogg, "Evolutionary History of the Grasses," vol. 125 of *Plant Physiology* (March 2001), 3.
6. Bruce R. McConkie, "Christ and the Creation," *Ensign*, June 1982, 11.
7. Gerald L. Schroeder, *God According to God* (New York: Harper One, 2009), 40.
8. Gould, *The Book of Life*, 7.
9. P.J. Gullan & P.S. Cranston, *The Insects* (West Sussex: Wiley-Blackwell, 2010), 4–5.
10. Gould, *The Book of Life*, 109.

8

OTHER CREATION
ACCOUNTS

The Creation is a very important event to us as members of The
Church of Jesus Christ of Latter-day Saints. A large part of our
temple worship, the endowment covenants, uses the Creation as the
vehicle or storyline for the covenants we make. The Creation gives us a
better understanding of the origin, need, and importance of those covenants. Thus, often when a member visits the temple, he or she reviews
yet again the events of the Creation and its effect on us today. Besides
Genesis, we have two more accounts of the Creation and other scriptures
that provide further information about it.

THE PEARL OF GREAT PRICE

There are entire commentaries about the *Pearl of Great Price* in which
scriptures from Genesis, Moses, and Abraham are compared verse by
verse, so that differences and similarities may be easily viewed.[1] Indeed,
these three accounts of the Creation are very similar. This is not surprising; Moses wrote the first two accounts himself. From the very similar wording in those accounts, it is likely that Abraham saw the same
vision as Moses and heard the same pronouncements of the Gods. But
Abraham included certain details that were either lost or never included

in Moses's account. It offers some slightly different perspectives that we should review. For example, there are several verses in the book of Abraham that have been used by critics as proofs that evolution could not have occurred. In a book like this, we would be remiss if we missed discussing those verses.

AFTER ITS OWN KIND—
ABRAHAM CHAPTER 4

The fourth chapter of Abraham can be confusing. The chapter heading indicates that in chapter 4, "The Gods plan the creation of the earth and all life thereon—Their plans for the six days of creation are set forth." Then in Abraham 5:4 we read that the Gods then carried out their plans with the statement that "the Gods came down and formed these the generations of the heavens and of the earth . . ." Some readers interpret chapter four as detailing the planning, or spiritual creation, of the earth and Abraham 5:4–21 as summarizing the physical creation.

With that preface, in the reading of the fourth chapter of Abraham, we read verses that seem to indicate that Abraham knew about the evolution debate that would occur millennia later and wanted to make his opinion known.

> And the Gods said: Let us prepare the earth to bring forth grass; the herb yielding seed; the fruit tree yielding fruit, *after his kind*, whose seed in itself *yieldeth its own likeness* upon the earth; and it was so, even as they ordered.
>
> And the Gods organized the earth to bring forth grass *from its own seed*, and the herb to bring forth herb *from its own seed*, yielding *seed after his kind*; and the earth to bring forth the tree *from its own seed*, yielding fruit, *whose seed could only bring forth the same in itself, after his kind*; and the Gods saw that they were obeyed. (Abraham 4:11–12, italics added)

When reading scriptures, it is often beneficial to question why the author worded particular verses the way he did. In the verses above, Abraham makes the point that fruit yielded fruit "after his kind" or similar expressions a total of *eight* times. Why? Why did Abraham place so much emphasis on the fact that apple trees yield apples and wheat yields more wheat?

Abraham then uses these phrases quite liberally again in the two verses describing the Lord's command of the earth to bring forth living animals.

> And the Gods prepared the earth to bring forth the living creature *after his kind*, cattle and creeping things, and beasts of the earth *after their kind*; and it was so, as they had said.
>
> And the Gods organized the earth to bring forth the beasts *after their kind*, and cattle *after their kind*, and every thing that creepeth upon the earth *after its kind*; and the Gods saw they would obey. (Abraham 4:24–25, italics added)

In these two verses, Abraham uses the phrase "after their kind" or "after its kind" *five* more times. As a successful herdsman (Genesis 13:2), Abraham had been around sheep and cattle his whole life. It would have been second nature to him—not even remotely questionable—that cattle birth cattle and sheep reproduce sheep. So why did Abraham feel the need to emphasize so strongly that the offspring of cattle would be more cattle and the offspring of beetles would be more beetles?

So, in total, within four short verses, Abraham used a phrase to indicate that plants and animals would only reproduce their own species a total of *thirteen* times. Why did he feel the need to stress the fact over and over in just a few verses? Why did he think there was even a possibility that life could be otherwise? Abraham did not know that an evolution debate would occur millennia later. A prophet does not make arguments for one side of a debate that has not even begun yet. There had to be another reason.

I propose the answer to that question is that Abraham had just seen a vision of millions of years of evolution in action. He had seen small one-celled algae evolve to become larger plants both in water and then on land. He saw plants became trees. Abraham had just seen the waters bring forth small fishes and then larger and more diversified sea creatures. In his vision, he had seen the earth bring forth small amphibians and then progressively larger reptiles and mammals. Though he may have known that the vision was a review of millions of years of history, it was probably one of the most confusing and disturbing revelations he ever witnessed in his role as prophet and seer. But then Abraham was able to calm down and put his vision in perspective. Abraham knew that he had never seen evolution in his normal life as a herdsman. Thus there had to be a difference is what had happened in the past and what was happening in his lifetime.

Thus, I propose, Abraham viewed evolution and this time period of the earth's history as the way that God had prepared or organized the earth for mankind. If Abraham had seen evolution from start to finish, he would have seen unrecognizable plant life develop into the grasses and trees with which he was familiar. He would have seen strange marine and land animals (such as dinosaurs) evolve into the fish, birds, and animal life, both wild and domesticated, that he recognized. But he could have interpreted the evolution part of the vision as simple preparation for the world with which he was familiar. These four verses (Abraham 4:1–2, 24–25) do not say that God brought forth the grass, herb, or cattle. It does say that He prepared the earth to do so. As long as evolution occurred as a part of the preparation and organization, it does not disagree with any of these verses.

Thus, it is not a stretch of the imagination to conclude that Abraham considered evolution as preparation and organization of the earth— since, in truth, that is exactly what evolution was. How better to prepare the earth than to bring forth the best grasses, fruits, and beasts by allowing them to evolve and improve over millions of years? Evolution is an optimizing function. The plants and animals best able to survive and thrive in their environment carry on their species. The weakest and least hardy die out. So, Abraham wrote,

> And the Gods organized the earth to bring forth grass from its own seed, and the herb to bring forth herb from its own seed, yielding seed after his kind. (Abraham 4:12)

I propose that we could interpret this verse as,

> And the Gods organized the earth *[so that it would be able]* to bring forth grass from its own seed, and the herb to bring forth herb from its own seed, yielding seed after his kind. (Abraham 4:12; italicized words added)

It seems that Abraham could have recognized that evolution was a preparatory step and the means used to organize the earth. But he also wanted to emphasize the fact that, with the arrival of Adam, evolution was not going to continue as it had in his vision of early creation. Thus he pointed out thirteen times in four verses that all plants and animals would only reproduce after their own kind once the preparation of the earth was done. But such overemphasis is common when the writer wants to make it very clear that a change has taken place. Abraham had no other reason to be so redundant about the fact that apple trees produce apples and cattle reproduce more cattle.

Taken that way, the book of Abraham actually *strengthens* the case for evolution. The fact that Abraham makes those thirteen statements about plant and animal reproduction indicates that Abraham was aware that there were times (spread over millions of years) that plants and animals did not reproduce exactly after their own kind. He had seen such a time through revelation. Actually, evolution has continued since the time of Adam, but not in the same ways as during the organization of the earth. For example, plant and animal breeders continue to use their skills to optimize the quality, disease resistance, and yield of the foods we eat. But in his vision Abraham had seen evolution throughout the entire earth over millions of years. He had then seen the change to his view of normalcy after the earth was fully prepared and organized. It was a change he wanted us to recognize and understand.

THE TEMPLE ENDOWMENT

As most Mormon readers will know, there are many parts of the temple ordinances which are not to be discussed outside of the temple itself. In the temple and through a series of temple ordinances, we make covenants for ourselves or, by proxy, for those people who have passed away. These ordinances have to be done in a certain order. The ordinance that takes the longest amount of time is called the endowment, where several covenants are made. As mentioned earlier, the endowment uses the Creation account as the vehicle or storyline for these covenants. The storyline is most often presented by film. When it comes time to make a covenant, the narrative is paused and the covenant is made.

The Creation story is ideal as the backdrop for such covenants. First, the purpose of the Creation of the earth is reviewed. Then the Creation of the earth is reenacted, thus setting the stage for the need and making of covenants. Interestingly, the temple account of the Creation is slightly different from the scriptural version. There is really no reason it shouldn't be different. There was a list of tasks that had to be accomplished for the earth to be prepared for mankind. In Genesis these tasks are lumped into six groupings. Though somewhat chronological, these six to-do lists overlapped considerably, as explained in earlier chapters. The temple endowment film simply groups the tasks a little differently. As explained by Bruce McConkie, "The Mosaic and Abrahamic accounts place the creative events on the same successive days . . . . The temple account, for reasons that are apparent to those familiar with its teachings, has a different division of events. It seems clear that the 'six days' are one continuing period and that there is no one place where the dividing lines between the successive events must of necessity be placed."[2]

There is yet another reason the temple endowment follows the Creation account. It was in the Garden of Eden, following God's plan and Adam and Eve's choices, that the relationship between earthly Man and God was established. Not insignificantly, the relationships between Man and Woman, Man and the earth, and, finally, Man and Satan were also set. Since our covenants need to be made with an understanding of these relationships and the purposes of earth life, the Creation story is an excellent means for both making the covenants and for understanding more about them each time one returns to the temple.

Finally, the temple endowment is set up to help us to better understand Adam and Eve and even relate to them a little better. Adam and Eve were given the most famous choice in the history of the world. Would they stay in the Garden of Eden or become mortal and live the more difficult, yet educational lives that earth life was meant to provide? By contemplating the choice made by Adam and Eve, we can better understand our purpose on earth, the difficulties we may find here, and why we need to remain faithful.

Notes

1. David J. Ridges, *Your Study of the Pearl of Great Price Made Easier* (Springville, UT: Cedar Fort, Inc, 2009).
2. Bruce R. McConkie, "Christ and the Creation," *Ensign*, June 1982, 11.

9

THE CREATION
OF MAN

For many faithful Church members, this may well be your least favorite chapter in the book. Of all of the narratives given us by the science of evolution, the creation of man is by far the hardest for people to accept. Most all of our teachings since childhood (and perhaps our own egos) tell us that man is special and was not created through the same means as were the beasts of the field. Evolutionists refute that belief, telling us that man evolved like the fish, birds, and animals. We are told that our evolutionary path went through the class of mammals and the order of primates. The data that supports the belief that man evolved continues to grow. Many Church members, including this author, have struggled mightily with this conflict of belief for years. The debate centers on the following scripture.

> And God said, Let us make man in our image, after our likeness: and let them have dominion over the fish of the sea, and over the fowl of the air, and over the cattle, and over all the earth, and over every creeping thing that creepeth upon the earth.
>
> So God created man in his *own* image, in the image of God created he him; male and female created he them. (Genesis 1:26–27)

So, it has been revealed who created Adam and we can calculate about when he was created. We even know why we were created for our mortal probation on earth. The mystery that fuels the creation-of-man debate is how Adam was created. Did Adam have earthly parents or not? Before proceeding further, it might be helpful to review the doctrine of the LDS Church in regard to the creation of Man. Many members believe and will categorically state that Church doctrine refutes all aspects of evolution. This is not, however, an accurate statement.

THE LDS CHURCH'S OFFICIAL POSITION ON THE CREATION OF MAN

In the debate between creationists and evolutionists within the LDS Church, there have been many speculations regarding the Church's official doctrine. William E. Evenson and Duane E. Jeffery wrote a short book on the subject titled *Mormonism and Evolution—The Authoritative LDS Statements*,[1] which summarized the history of all Church statements on the matter.

In 1909, the First Presidency of Joseph F. Smith first published an official statement regarding evolution. In a nutshell, the statement reviewed established doctrine that there was a spiritual creation before a physical creation and that Adam was created in the image of God. Then the statement concludes.

> It is held by some that Adam was not the first man upon this earth, and that the original human being was a development from lower orders of the animal creation. These, however, are the theories of men. The word of the Lord declares that Adam was "the first man of all men" (Moses 1:34) and we are therefor in duty bound to regard him as the primal parent of our race.

In 1930, Elder Joseph Fielding Smith, then a junior member of the Quorum of the Twelve, delivered a talk at a conference of the Genealogical Society of Utah. In it, he stated that human life did not exist upon the earth prior to Adam and that there was no death upon the earth prior to the fall of man. B. H. Roberts, then senior president of the Seventy, submitted a letter of objection to the First Presidency of Heber J. Grant, asking if the views of Elder Smith were to be considered Church doctrine or if he was putting forth his own opinions on the matter. Elder Roberts and Elder Smith both appeared before the Quorum of the Twelve to plead their cases. The matter was passed on to the First Presidency. In their response, Heber J. Grant and his counselors supported Joseph F. Smith's 1909 statement that "Adam is the primal parent of our race." They did not, however, support President Joseph Fielding Smith's declarations that there was no death before the Fall or that pre-Adamites never existed. Instead, in a memo to the other general authorities of the Church, President Grant declared that it was not the responsibility or calling of the Church to try to answer this question.

> Our mission is to bear the message of the restored gospel to the people of the world. Leave Geology, Biology, Archeology, and Anthropology, no one of which has to do with the salvation of the souls of mankind to, to scientific research . . .

In the same memo, President Grant stated,

> The statement made by Elder Smith that the existence of pre-Adamites is not a doctrine of the church is true. It is just as true that the statement, "There were not pre-Adamites upon the earth," is not a doctrine of the church. Neither side of the controversy has been accepted as a doctrine at all.[1]

President Grant thus changed the Church's stance on evolution from pro-creationist to complete neutrality. Adam was the first "man" on earth, but the Church would not take an official position on how his body got here. To demonstrate the neutrality of the Church on the subject, Elder James E. Talmage was allowed to give a talk on evolution in the Tabernacle. His talk was published in *Church News* (Nov. 1931) and later in a pamphlet published by the Church. Though Elder Talmage does not advocate that Adam was related to the primates, his talk was decidedly pro-evolution and he recognized that pre-Adamites did exist.

> Geologists say that these very simple forms of plant and animal bodies were succeeded by others more complicated . . . . In due course came the crowning work of this creative sequence, the advent of man!" Geologists and anthropologists say that if the beginning of Adamic history dates back but 6000 years or less, there must have been races of human sort upon the earth long before that time.[1]

In 1954, Joseph Fielding Smith, now a senior apostle and still an advocate for creationism, published *Man: His Origin and Destiny*, where he wrote, "There were no peoples of any sort upon the earth before Adam. The doctrines of "pre-Adamites" is not a doctrine of the Church and is not advocated or countenanced in the Church." In response to the many questions as to whether the book now represented the Church's official position, President David O. McKay disavowed the book as representing Church doctrine, writing, "On the subject of organic evolution, the Church has officially taken no position. [The book] expresses the views of the author, for which he assumes full responsibility."[1]

It is noteworthy that when Joseph Fielding Smith became the President of the Church in 1970, he could have probably changed the official Church position. The prophet of the Church can, after all, initiate changes in established Church doctrine. But he chose not to do so. In regard to Church doctrine, our Church leadership has wisely chosen to leave the matter unresolved. Some past scholars and leaders of the Church have spoken out against the existence of pre-Adamites and evolution.[2,3] Despite those talks and the perceptions of many Saints, the Church does not take sides in the creationist/evolutionist debate. Members are encouraged to believe as they will. In a paper he prepared for the *Ensign*, President Spencer W. Kimball wrote, "Man became a living soul—mankind, male and female. The Creators breathed into their nostrils the breath of life, and man and woman became living souls. We don't know exactly how their coming into this world happened, and when we're able to understand it the Lord will tell us."[4] In an interview which included a question on evolution, President Gordon B. Hinckley summarized the Church's present doctrine: "What the church requires is only belief that Adam was the first man of what we would call the human race."[5]

TAKING GENESIS LITERALLY

So there are two possible scenarios for the creation of Adam and Eve. In the first, we take the scriptures very literally. First, God "formed man of the dust of the ground." One might picture God sculpting Adam's body out of mud on a raised platform. Or one might picture that God magically formed Adam and he rose directly out of the ground beneath his feet. Then it became Eve's turn for creation.

> And the Lord God caused a deep sleep to fall upon Adam, and he slept: and he took one of his ribs, and closed up the flesh instead thereof;
> And the rib, which the Lord God had taken from man, made he a woman, and brought her unto the man. (Genesis 2:21–22)

Thus one might picture the Lord actually removing Adam's rib from his side. We could think it magically sprang forth to become a woman, our mother Eve. With these scenarios, both Adam's and Eve's creations would have involved a significant application of godly power and neither would have been through natural means.

Or one might believe that the accounts of the creation of Adam and Eve were largely symbolic. Man was formed from the dust such that we would understand the temporary nature of this life. Adam was *not* made from granite, a more permanent form of the ground on which we stand. He was made of dust, the most fleeting type of ground. Adam was made from dust so that he (and we) would come to understand that he would eventually "return unto the ground; for out of it wast thou taken: for dust thou art, and unto dust shalt thou return" (Genesis 3:19).

We might also recognize that the creation of Eve was just as symbolic as her husband's. Eve was created from one of Adam's ribs. How better to communicate the relationship of man to woman? Adam himself immediately recognizes the meaning when he states,

> And Adam said, This is now bone of my bones, and flesh of my flesh: she shall be called Woman, because she was taken out of Man.
> Therefore shall a man leave his father and his mother, and shall cleave unto his wife: and they shall be one flesh. (Genesis 2:23–24)

How better to recognize how a married couple should feel toward each other? We are only in the second chapter of Genesis and we are being given a lesson on the importance of unity in marriage. A man and his wife are to be *one*. Matthew Henry (1662–1714), a Presbyterian minister who wrote several commentaries on the Bible, found even greater symbolism in the Lord's rib metaphor.

> The woman was made of a rib out of the side of Adam; not made out of his head to rule over him, nor out of his feet to be trampled upon

by him, but out of his side to be equal with him, under his arm to be protected, and near his heart to be beloved.[6]

This comment was both beautifully poetic and true.

On a side note, Adam's wording in Genesis 2:24 is very interesting in that Adam recognizes that a man must leave his earthly father and mother to cleave unto his wife. But if Adam had been created from the dust of the earth, he wouldn't have had an earthly father and mother to leave! In fact, there would have been no fathers or mothers on the earth at all yet. But if Adam and Eve had descended from pre-Adamites, they would have each had a mother and father. Only if Adam's body was a son of earthly parents would Adam's statement make any sense.

WHAT IS A "MAN"?

There are two main difficulties in comparing what the scriptures teach us and what evolution tells us. As we have just discussed, there is the problem of recognizing symbolism in the scriptural account. Was Adam literally sculpted from the dust of the earth? Was Eve actually made from one of Adam's ribs? Was Satan actually a serpent? Secondly, we once again have a problem with the simple definition of words. As discussed earlier, what is a "day," "morning" and "evening," or "light" and "darkness"? What is a "firmament" and what "waters" are being divided? At this point, we need to address the definition of the word "man." In Genesis 1:26, God stated his intention to "make man in our image, after our likeness." In chapter 2, He accomplishes that task.

> And the Lord God formed man of the dust of the ground, and breathed into his nostrils the breath of life; and man became a living soul. (Genesis 2:7)

Man became a living soul. What is a living soul? As defined by Doctrine and Covenants 88:15, "And the spirit and the body are the soul of man." Thus a "Man," by definition, is the union between a spirit child of our Heavenly Father and a body of flesh and bones. Since Adam was the first to become a living soul, he was also the first man, by the definition of man that God has given us. Thus to call pre-Adamites "men" is a misnomer and has caused a lot of confusion in discussions about Genesis.

In fact, much of the argument between evolutionists and creationists seems to be due to simple semantics. Evolutionary biologists and archeologists use the term "man" to describe prehistoric pre-Adamites that are not that far removed from the primates. Biblically, the word "man" is only used to describe Adam, Eve, and their descendants. In this discussion, we will use the latter definition. God declared that Adam was the first man in Genesis 1:26, so we will honor that definition. We will use the general term "pre-Adamites" to describe the hominids that existed before Adam.

As mentioned earlier, President Gordon B. Hinckley stated, "What the church requires is only belief that Adam was the first man of what we would call the human race." That is not a problem. Adam, by the correct definition of "man," was the first man. But this fact does not preclude the possibility that there were pre-Adamites, hominids, or prehistoric man-*like* beings, on the earth as well, both before and during the time of Adam. These pre-Adamites did not possess the spirits of Heavenly Father's children. But, to my knowledge, there is not a single verse in the scriptures that indicates such man-like beings didn't exist. Since we now have a great deal of fossil and genetics evidence that prehistoric man-like beings *did* exist, we must at least consider the possibility.

AN EVOLUTIONARY CREATION OF ADAM

To reconcile the scriptural and evolutionary accounts, we need to consider that the Lord never stated that he created animal life on the sixth day. As discussed in chapter 7 (and Moses 2), the creator commands, "Let the earth bring forth the living creature after his kind . . ." The wording of this command is conducive to the idea that this was a command to earth to initiate and then continue the process of evolution. This command was obeyed and the earth did bring forth living creatures. The smartest group of creatures brought forth was the primates.

The fossil record indicates that pre-Adamites existed as long as 3.5 million years ago, long before the creation of Adam. *Australopithecus afarensis* was the first of these species, whose fossils were found, despite the name, in Africa. *Homo rudolfensis, Homo robustus, Homo boisei,*

Homo erectus and several other primate species made their appearances and then their disappearances. *Homo neanderthalensis*, or Neanderthals, the last of the truly prehistoric pre-Adamites with characteristics between those of apes and men, appeared about 200,000 years ago. So-called "Modern Man" (which by our definition of man is still a misnomer) or *Homo sapiens* had skeletal characteristics the same as ours today and appeared about 70,000–100,000 years ago in Africa. About 60,000 years ago, *Homo sapiens* emigrated to Europe and overlapped with Neanderthals for about 30,000 years. Then 30,000 years ago, for reasons unknown, Neanderthals became extinct and Homo sapiens continued. The fossil record indicates that these pre-Adamites made and used tools, wore clothes, built homes and villages, drew pictures on the walls of caves, and used fire.

To resolve the discrepancies between the evolution and scriptural accounts, we now must extrapolate a bit. There is really only one way to get the evolutionary and scriptural account timelines to line up. About 6,000 years ago, the bodies of the man Adam and the woman Eve would have been adult members of a tribe of pre-Adamites. *Homo sapiens* had finally evolved to the point that our Heavenly Father judged them ready and worthy to house His spirit children for their brief sojourn on Earth. It was time to start the whole process of mortal life. In 4000 BC, about when we believe that Adam and Eve were created, there was a world population of seven million people.[7] Out of that population, Heavenly Father chose one male to be Adam and one female to be Eve. Into them He breathed the breath of life and "man became a living soul."

Adam and Eve then had to move eastward to spend some time in the Garden of Eden. We don't know how long they were there, but if Eve had come from a community of other people, she would have probably realized within a few months that she and Adam were not having children. This realization may have been the trigger for her to listen to Satan and start the process of the fall. In any case, the fall occurred and Adam and Eve were forced to move out of the Garden of Eden. They may well have moved back into the community from which they came. It would have been a logical recourse.

This account may be unsettling for many. But we don't have a historical, non-symbolic account of how Adam's body was created. Thus this evolutionary account does not contradict any scriptures of which I am aware. It is an explanation of how Adam and Eve came to be that blends together the evidence of the sciences with the account of the scriptures.

ADAM'S NEIGHBORS

From archeological evidence, carbon dating of tools made by pre-Adamites, and extrapolating back from known population counts, it has been calculated that there were about 7,000,000 people on earth at the time of Adam and Eve. What happened to the other 6,999,998 people? There is no record of a colossal extermination of everyone else. Actually, there is no evidence that anything happened to those people. They continued to live.

This population of pre-Adamites does clear up certain otherwise troublesome verses in the Old Testament.

1. If God created Adam from the dust, why not just have created him in the Garden of Eden instead of moving them there later? (Genesis 2:8)
2. Neither Adam nor Eve expressed surprise that Satan shows up in the Garden in the third chapter of Genesis or in the temple account. If they were the only beings on the earth, wouldn't the appearance of a stranger have been confusing for them and worthy of a question?
3. The presence of seven million other people means that Adam and Eve's children didn't have to marry their own brothers and sisters, an incestuous act that would soon be forbidden under the Mosaic law.
4. In Genesis 4:15, the Lord set a mark upon Cain, to warn anyone finding him from deciding to kill him. Would that have been necessary if everyone else on the earth had been a close relative to Cain and would have known him on sight? A few verses later, shortly after being exiled from the rest of his family for murdering Able, Cain "builded a city" called Enoch in the land of Nod (Genesis 4:17). Who lived there? Cain, his wife, and a few children could hardly have made up a city. But, if there were seven million people on the earth, Cain could

certainly have found enough people to populate his city in a short amount of time.

So, were the children of these other 6,999,998 pre-Adamites still creatures of evolution or were they men, housing the spirit children of our Heavenly Father? Again, we can only speculate. The idea that Adam is the "father of all mankind" could be figurative. We know that Adam and Eve were evicted from the Garden of Eden and had to make their way out into the world. As Adam and Eve's descendants continued to spread throughout the land, most would have married outside of the immediate family. But in doing so, their children would all have been descendants of Adam and, thus, should also be living souls. It would take a number of generations, but gradually Adam's seed would have spread to all parts of the world, inserting themselves into the families of the earth. So figuratively or literally, we have all become Adam's children.

However, as far as the evolutionary sciences are concerned, nothing of importance happened 6,000 years ago. The spirits of men do not leave a fossil record. But the Old Testament gives us enough detail about the generations that followed Adam and certain key events that were dated in other historical records for us to do the math and determine that Adam and Eve had to have lived about 6,000 years ago, in approximately 4000 BC. We also have the evolutionary account of what was happening on Earth in the same time period. This combined scriptural/evolutionary narrative is speculative, but it does allow one to reconcile the two accounts of the beginning of man.

THE FINDINGS OF
GENETICS RESEARCH

Many of the topics discussed so far have been parts of debates that have gone on for a couple hundred years. Findings in the field of genetics and discussions around them have only occurred in the last few decades.

As a quick review of our genetic structure, our DNA is contained within 23 double-helix structures called chromosomes. Within those 23 chromosomes, we have about 20,000 genes,[8] which create the proteins needed by our cells and bodies to function and maintain life. As explained in chapter 6, those genes and all the connecting segments of DNA between them are made up of pairs of four organic molecules called base pairs. The molecular bonds of these linkages are curved in such a way to force each molecule to gradually spiral around the other, causing the double helix. Incredibly, there are about 3 billion base pairs in our genome. When geneticists sequence your DNA, they are simply determining the order of these base pairs. The results of the sequencing may look something like "CCTGAGGAAATT . . ." Your DNA string is very long, but also rather boring since you only get to use four letters and no words will be discernable.

Long before genetic sequencing became common practice, genetics research had made comparisons of our DNA structure to that of other species. First, the chromosomes of all plants and animals (except bacteria) have the same double-helix structure that we do. Secondly, all plants and animals (including bacteria) have genes within those chromosomes, just like we do. Lastly, all genes are made up of the same four nucleotide base pairs that we have. Naturally, these similarities suggested that humans, plants, and animals all have a common ancestor. It seemed unlikely that every species on Earth could have been created individually or evolved separately, yet still have the same basic DNA structure of nucleotides, genes, and double helixes. Years ago we knew DNA from these various species was chemically very similar. Yet, mainly due to the religious implications of such a conclusion, the general public was not ready to accept anything but incontrovertible proof of man's evolution. Not until the technology was developed to fully sequence our genes and conduct a molecule-by-molecule comparison with other plant and animal species could we know how very similar we are to the rest of Earth's plant, bacterial, and animal life.

Obviously there are some differences in the DNA of different species—or there would be no differences between the species and we would all look alike. Since chromosomes can break and reform, the number of chromosomes varies between species. As stated, humans have 23 pairs of chromosomes. But a fruit fly has four pairs of chromosomes, a rice plant has 12 pairs, and a dog has 39 pairs.[7] Active genes can both duplicate themselves and add to their number or be inactivated and reduce their number. So different species have varying numbers of genes as well.

Humans have about 20,000 genes in our makeup. But chickens have about 17,000 genes and grapes have over 30,000.[9]

So what has happened in the last few decades to change the evolution/creationist debate? Simply put, the instruments that sequence DNA have gotten much faster at their jobs, sparking a new era in genetics research. It became possible to sequence the human genome in a matter of years instead of centuries. The Human Genome Project was completed in 2003, when all the base-pair building blocks of human DNA were sequenced.[10] From earlier and concurrent research, many segments of this code were identified as the specific genes that shape our bodies and allow them to function correctly. Researchers could finally link genetic code with genetic functions. Much has been learned since then. Geneticists are even figuring out how to remove genetic flaws from fertilized eggs, before those flaws have a chance to express themselves into handicaps for the unborn child.[11] The potential for good of such research is incredible. Genetics analysis has now become inexpensive and commonplace. For a few dollars, you can send in some of your cells and determine your bloodlines. How much Nordic, Asian, or American Indian DNA do you have in you? Using the same type of DNA analysis and comparison, geneticists are starting to relate the history of the human race.[12]

OUR GENETIC SIMILARITY TO BANANAS AND OTHER SPECIES

As fast sequencing of the individual base pairs in DNA became achievable, comparing the similarity of the DNA of different species became the new argument for evolution. It turned out to be quite a convincing argument as well. Since the "alphabet" of DNA only contains four letters (C, T, A, and G), some similarity is expected. But with three billion or so base pairs to compare, similarity above and beyond random chance is going to be obvious. To start with, when you compare your DNA to that of your neighbor, you will find that 99.9% of your sequences are a match.[13] If you are related to your neighbor, the percentage goes up even more.

But you also share about 24% of your genes with rice[14] and about 60% of your DNA with bananas.[15] Comparing ourselves within the animal kingdom, about 70% of your DNA sequence is similar to that of a zebrafish.[16] As one might expect, similarity increases as we move our comparisons to within the mammalian class. We share about 84% of the same DNA sequences as a dog and 85% of the DNA of a cow. About 88% of our DNA is similar to the DNA of a mouse.[14] You can probably see where this is going and it should not surprise you that as we move into the order of primates we find the most DNA similarity. About 97% of our DNA nucleotide sequencing is the same as the gorilla.[13] But at the top of the human DNA similarity list is the chimpanzee. When you lay the DNA sequences of man next to that of chimpanzees, fully 99% of the base pairs match.[17] While 99% sounds like a large percentage (and it is), it still does not really reflect the level of similarity between human and chimpanzee. To understand how that is possible, one needs to understand that our genetic sequences are not nearly as stable as we once believed.[18]

Geneticists have known for many years that genes can mutate, which introduces changes in all future generations of the mutant. Most of these mutations are due to a loss, addition, or a substitution of only a single base pair. Often genes can work around such small changes in their makeup and continue functioning. But other mutations can involve large segments of dozens of base pairs. It has been found that segments of DNA, rather descriptively called "jumping genes," can be extracted from their places and moved to a completely different location in the chromosome. Long segments of DNA base pairs can also be copied by a strand of RNA, which then builds that DNA copy into yet another location of the genome.[18] Geneticists can trace back where the jumping genes and self-copying genes came from and went to. To come up with the interspecies similarities quoted above, correction is made for the gene-swapping changes that can be proven. For example, if these corrections are not made, then our DNA is only 96% identical to chimpanzees.[17]

When such major mutations occur, any genes from which these DNA segments are cut (and into which they are inserted) cannot generally recover from such drastic resequencing and they become non-functional. Generally, our cells each have several copies of the same gene in our genome, so losing one of those copies is not catastrophic. But other times our cells may have only one such gene. When it has been rendered useless due to mutation, we can lose very useful abilities. For example, early in our evolutionary progress, it appears that we lost the genes that enabled us to produce our own Vitamin C. Many mammal species still have that ability, but we don't. Since our progenitors consumed enough fruits to provide them with Vitamin C, the loss of the gene was not fatal. But its loss is still a genetic deficiency. Today, if you don't get enough Vitamin C in your diet, you will get scurvy and eventually die. Obviously such major mutations are very rare events. Fortunately, we could afford to lose the gene that allows us to make our own Vitamin C, as long as we have that vitamin in our diets. But many similar genes losses are fatal; we never see examples of many mutations because the mutation causes early death or sterility.

When a mutation causes a gene to become dysfunctional, it becomes what is called a pseudogene. A pseudogene looks like a normal gene, but it simply doesn't function any longer. Gene duplication actually helps geneticists to date mutations and follow the genetic linkages of different species. Let's say, for example, that early in our primate heritage a gene successfully duplicated itself, inserting its exact copy in the next neighborhood of its chromosome. But the gene copy's neighborhood is in a state of constant flux. Base pairs move in and out. Several major insertions and deletions of base pairs finally render the copied gene inactive and it becomes a pseudogene. But the mutations continue. Now, a few millions of year later, a geneticist studying the DNA sequences of this primate notices the similarity of the still-active gene and the inactive pseudogene copy. In a side-by-side comparison, the geneticist can identify and count the number of mutations that have occurred in the pseudogene, mutations that cannot have occurred in the active gene or it would no longer be active. Knowing approximately how often such mutations happen, the geneticist can approximate when the gene duplication occurred. If two different species of primates have the same active gene and inactive pseudogene in the same part of their chromosomes, then the gene duplication happened before the species split apart from one another. If one of the two species has only the active gene, then the duplication happened after the split of the two species. Going back to our earlier example, neither primates nor humans can synthesize their own Vitamin C, though dogs, cats and other mammals can. Our loss of the Vitamin C-synthesizing gene occurred after our primate's genetic line broke off from other mammals.[18]

It was stated earlier that, while 96–99% similarity in base pair sequence is a very large percentage, it still understates how similar humans and chimpanzees are. Because not only do the base pair sequences of the active genes match, the DNA in between those genes lines up, and the sequences of the pseudogenes are also highly similar. Thus, most of the mutations that caused our pseudogenes to lose their functionality happened before the split of humans from chimpanzees and are found in the same chromosomal location of both species. The same exact mutations and pseudogene creations would not have occurred in each species independently—mutations are too random. Only the few more recent mutations, which occurred after the split of the human line from the chimpanzee line (about 3.5 million years ago), are found in one species but not the other.

For decades, many faithful Christians like myself were able to accept the basic tenets of evolution, but drew the line at accepting that Adam descended through the animal kingdom and the family of primates. This last concession was too much in conflict with what has been taught in our churches since Darwin first reluctantly proposed the idea of evolution.

A METAPHOR— CARBON VERSUS DIAMOND

To help in your reconciliation of the concept of Adam and Eve's evolution, allow me to offer a metaphor. Coal and diamond are both made up of exactly the same element—carbon. A lump of coal is a black, soft rock which breaks and easily rubs off coal dust onto your hands. But if you take a lump of coal and put it under extreme pressure and temperature for many years, that lump of coal will become a diamond. There is no danger of mistaking the new diamond for another lump of coal.

The diamond is clear, very hard, and significantly more valuable. Once sculpted, very few people would despise a beautiful diamond because it still has the same elemental makeup of a lowly chunk of coal. The coal has been refined to become a new substance in which we can delight.

Thus it is with our bodies, which have been through an evolutionary refining process of their own. Do our prehistoric origins matter that much? Both fossil and genetic evidence indicates that our human bodies passed through an evolutionary process. For many, this has been a difficult finding to accept. But we should consider the reasons behind that reluctance. If our ancestors were primates and before that smaller mammals, does that fact make our bodies today any less amazing? How would it somehow be better if Adam had been molded from the clay? Through evolution, God has developed the ultimate vehicle for our spirits to use while going through this earthly probation. The last step of the perfection process, going from primate to man, took about 3.5 million years. We are now a species with no equal. Our minds have continued to elevate us to be able to provide a quality of life unknown to past generations. We have unlimited art, literature, and information at our fingertips. But should we be so proud of whom we are today that we deny what we are learning about our origins? Without a doubt, our bodies are more amazing that any man-made construction and more precious than diamonds, no matter where they might have originated.

WHY ARE HUMANS
SO SPECIAL?

The Church teaches us that humans *are* special. But we have to consider for a moment why we are special. After all, our bodies are much like those of any of the other mammals. We all have hair and red blood. Our respiratory, circulatory, and digestive systems are similar to the animals. Our females give birth to our children and nurse their young with milk. We are the smartest of the mammals, but we are not the biggest, the fastest, nor the strongest. When we die, our bodies disintegrate into the earth like any other mammal. We share about 97% of our DNA with the other primates, which is not that surprising as we compare our hands, facial structures, and body construction to theirs. So, why should we consider man so special?

One of the best-known songs in the LDS Church is "I am a Child of God." We teach this song to our Primary children so they are aware from an early age that they are children of loving earthly parents, yet they are also children of a loving Heavenly Father. From that song, we can learn that Man is special because we each have a special spirit child of our Heavenly Father that resides in our specialized body. The body is an extraordinary vehicle for the spirit. But it is a vehicle that wears out in this life. Like a car with too many miles on it, that vehicle will need to be replaced in the resurrection. Though we need the body to attain our perfect form (Alma 11:43), it is only a part of us. It is a vehicle for our spirits. Again, let it be known that our bodies are wonderful vehicles with the mental abilities and manual dexterity to manipulate the world around us. Evolved or created, our bodies are better than anything Mercedes-Benz could produce. But it is still a vehicle and the suggestion that our body evolved over time should not really upset us that much. Since Adam, we are souls and that makes us unique of all God's creations.

A FINAL THOUGHT

Archeologists tell us that 6,000 years ago, evolution brought about pre-Adamites who looked and acted much like men today, who wore clothes, used tools, lived in villages, created art on cave walls, and used fire. These pre-Adamites shared 99.9% of our DNA. Does it really make sense that God went ahead anyway and created new bodies "from the dust" for Adam and Eve that were so identical to the pre-Adamites as to be indistinguishable? Would God have gone through such obvious redundancy just so mankind would not have to bear the shame of being descendants of the animals?

In conclusion, there is much evidence that mankind is the culmination of an evolutionary process. But no offense should be taken in that conclusion. To look at it another way, all of the elements in our bodies were first created in suns—but we are not suns. All the water in our bodies was once part of a vast ocean—but we are not oceans either. In our digestive systems, we have millions of bacteria that help us process our food—but we are not bacteria. Finally, until our species split off in its own direction, our bodies may have initially evolved through the same evolutionary path of other primates; yet, if they did, we are not monkeys. We are mankind. It does not matter from where the elements, water, or the DNA in our bodies originated. We have a spirit inside of each of us that is a child of our Heavenly Father and that is what makes us special and unique.

NOTES

1. William E Evenson & Duane E. Jeffery, *Mormonism and Evolution: The Authoritative LDS Statements* (Salt Lake City: Greg Kofford Books, 2005).
2. Joseph Fielding McConkie, *Answers: Straightforward Answers to Tough Gospel Questions* (Salt Lake City: Deseret Book, 1998) 158–162.
3. Robert J. Matthews, "The Fall of Man" in *The Man Adam* (Salt Lake City: Bookcraft, 1990) 54.
4. Spencer W. Kimball, "The Blessings and Responsibilities of Womanhood," *Ensign*, March 1976.
5. Evenson & Jeffery, *Mormonism and Evolution*, 111.
6. *Matthew Henry's Commentary on the Whole Bible.*
7. Colin McEvedy and Richard Jones, *Atlas of World Population History* (New York: Facts on File, 1979), 344.
8. "Chromosomes," Nation Human Genome Research Institute, https://www.genome.gov/26524120/chromosomes-fact-sheet.
9. Mihaela Pertea & Steven L. Salzberg, "Between a chicken and a grape: estimating the number of human genes," Genome *Biol.* 2010; 11(5): 206: accessed at https://www.ncbi.nlm.nih.gov/pmc/articles/PMC2898077/
10. "A Brief History: From Mendel to the Human Genome Project," *Genome: Unlocking Life's Code*: https://unlockinglifescode.org/timeline?tid=4.
11. Steve Connor, "First Human Embryos Edited in U.S." MIT Technology Review, July 26, 2017.
12. Sean B. Carroll, *The Making of the Fittest* (New York: W. W. Norton, 2006).
13. Bill Nye, *Undeniable* (New York: St. Martin's Press, 2014), 247, 259.
14. "Genes Are Us. And Them." *National Geographic*, Vol. 224 #1 (July 2013), 102.

15. "2010 Nation DNA Day Online Chatroom Transcript," Nation Human Genome Research Insititute: https://www.genome.gov/dnaday/q.cfm?aid =785&year=2010.

16. Kersten Howe, "The Zebrafish Reference Genome Sequence and Its Relationship to the Human Genome" *Nature*. Apr. 2013; 496(7446): 498– 503; accessed at https://www.ncbi.nlm.nih.gov/pmc/articles/PMC3703927.

17. "Initial Sequence of the Chimpanzee Genome and Comparison with the Human Genome" by The Chimpanzee Sequencing an Analysis Consortium, *Nature*, vol. 437 (Sept 2005); accessed at https://www.genome .gov/15515096/2005-release-new-genome-comparison-finds-chimps -humans-very-similar-at-dna-level.

18. Daniel J. Fairbanks, *Relics of Eden* (Amherst, NY: Prometheus Books, 2007), 53–54.

10

NOAH'S ARK—A
GLOBAL FLOOD?

n the preceding chapters, we have endeavored to reconcile the religious
and the scientific stories of the Creation. But, besides the Creation
account, new findings of the last century have challenged many of our
perceptions of the other Old Testament stories as well. Some of those
challenges have convincing, significant proofs behind them that we need
to address. If we can't find a good response to the challenge of our beliefs,
we may have to adjust our perceptions. The story of Noah's Ark is a good
example of a teaching that begs for review.

Many of our mental images and perceptions about our Old
Testament accounts are actually hundreds of years old, first described by
thought leaders in the earliest days of the Catholic Church. At that time,
there was no data from archeology or the other sciences to shed light on
these Old Testament accounts. These church leaders gave their own view
of the scriptures, many of which were based on how they interpreted just
a few words. But these ideas were taught to hundreds of generations, so
those interpretations have endured well over the centuries.

After the Creation account and the tragic story of Cain and Abel,
the next Old Testament narrative we read is about Noah's Ark, as found
in Genesis chapters 6–9. The Noah's Ark narrative has received much
ridicule over the years. Stand-up comics have reenacted God's first

communication with Noah to build an ark on land. The idea of gathering all the animals on the planet (even those separated by vast oceans) seems absurd. Thus many people have come to look at the story of Noah's Ark as a work of fiction included in the Bible to teach us that God will save the lives of righteous men—even if that means flooding the whole earth.

Science cannot resolve whether or not Noah's Ark was fact or fiction. But, just like the Creation story, science can help us better interpret the scriptural account. In this case, it is the field of geology that better defines our understanding of this Genesis narrative. The history of geology and the account of Noah's flood are very intertwined. As David Montgomery described in his book, *The Rocks Don't Lie*,

> The initial development of the discipline of geology was premised on the Flood as fact, which naturally led to imaginative theories on how to interpret the story of Noah's Flood. Later, with evidence literally in their hands and beneath their feet, geologists began to influence theology, showing that a global flood fell short when tested against the rocks that make up our world.[1]

The debate on Noah's Flood started as far back as 1666. Even then it was realized that there was simply not enough water on the earth to totally flood its surface. An Anglican bishop man named Edward Stillingfleet calculated that all the world's clouds would not have provided nearly enough water to flood the earth.[2] Thus Stillingfleet and many of his contemporaries opted to believe that Noah's Ark was built for a regional, not a global, flood. But the lack of enough water to flood the whole earth's surface was a subject of debate for many years. A Jesuit scholar named Athanasius Kircher published a book in 1674 in which he proposed that, to cause Noah's Flood, God had caused large underground lakes to overflow.[3] According to Kircher's theory, with the draining of these underground lakes, some of the earth's unsupported crust collapsed, leaving the earth's surface the way we see it today. No evidence of such vast underground lakes was ever found, but the theory is still purported in Bible-study groups even today. The point of this little bit of history is to point out that the belief that Noah's flood could have been a regional flood in Mesopotamia and not a truly global flood, has existed for over three centuries. Nevertheless, the debate continues even today.

Much of the study of earth's history through geology is made possible by the fact that ocean floors are continuously covered by silt, dirt, sediment, and the bodies of fish and other marine life that have died in the waters above. Over time, due to the pressures above them, these layers harden and become stratified layers of rock. Due to continental drift and massive upheavals of the earth's surface, many of these ocean floors have been raised above the water's surface, often forming large mountain ranges in the process.

One of the best places to examine such rock layers is the Grand Canyon. Before there was a canyon there, the area was part of a vast ocean that covered much of the western half of the United States. Over millions of years, layers of sediment formed and hardened. Then, about 270 million years ago, a massive earthquake and upheaval raised this ocean floor up to become dry land. Those rock layers, bearing in them fossils and the history of that ocean, remained hidden underground. But in northwest Arizona, a large river decided to run through the land. Now called the Colorado River, it has eroded and sliced through those rock layers for about five million years. The Grand Canyon is a mile deep and exposes these multi-colored layers for easy examination by geologists and appreciation by tourists. Through analysis, each layer has been dated, so we have a natural geological time line for reference any time we like. The Grand Canyon is much older than Noah's Ark and none of its layers are as recent as 2300 BC. But other natural and man-made excavations do display layers deposited in that era.

Let us now imagine the effects of a global flood that one would expect to see in excavated layers of earth that were deposited in lake and sea-bottoms 4,300 years ago. With a global flood, millions of tons of dirt would have been eroded off of the dry land and into the lakes and oceans. According to Genesis, this sediment would have had almost a year to homogenize, spread around the earth, and gradually settle in the lowest points of the entire world (oceans, lakes and canyons). This sediment layer would have been extraordinarily thick and strewn with the fossils of the millions of dead animals and birds killed in the Flood. If Noah's Flood was truly global, a very thick, unique, and easily recognizable sediment layer would have been found in any formations that dated to about 2300 BC.

However, there is no such sediment layer anywhere. There is simply no evidence that a global flood ever occurred. As mentioned earlier, this lack of evidence was not due to a lack of trying on the part of early geologists. Most of them were very faithful and religious men, early geologists who looked for and fully expected to find evidence of Noah's Flood. There have been many claims that evidence of Noah's Ark has been found. But, under more stringent examination, all such claims have been found to be false. Here are just a few more challenges to the story of Noah's Ark that require explanation.

1. As mentioned, there is simply not enough water on the earth to flood the whole surface of the earth. Then there is also the question of where the flood waters would have gone after the flood was over. In the search for oil, we have now mapped out the contents of most of the world beneath our feet. The vast underground caverns of water proposed by Athanasius Kircher simply do not exist.

2. Just in his homeland of Mesopotamia, Noah would have had a large number of native animal species to save. But a global flood would demand that he also save all the animal species found in North America, South America, Australia, Africa, Asia, and even Antarctica. Thus, Noah would have had to fit millions of species of insects, rodents, birds, reptiles, and mammals onto his Ark, which would have required a much larger ark. Also problematic is explaining how those species native to other continents returned to their homes without leaving fossil evidence or offspring during the long migration to Mesopotamia or back home again.

3. Finally, there is the problem regarding the population of the world. As mentioned in chapter 9, at the time of Adam, there were approximately 7 million people on the earth. By the time of Noah, it is estimated that there were about 20 million people on the earth.[4] A global flood would have killed them all. That would have started the evolution of Man all over again. Our population would have had only 6,000 years to diversify again. This is not nearly enough time for mankind to develop the racial diversity we see today. As David Montgomery put it, "Could Pygmies, Vikings, and Aborigines all have descended

from Noah in just a few thousand years, when classical statues revealed that Greeks and Italians look the same way two thousand years ago as they do today?"[5]

DO THE SCRIPTURES ACTUALLY REQUIRE A GLOBAL FLOOD?

At this point in the evaluation process, you should be going back to your scriptures to see what amount of flexibility there may be regarding this new data. Again, much of this debate may be semantics. There is one phrase upon which the global flood proponents base their argument. The verses with that phrase are as follows.

> Genesis 6:1—And it came to pass, when men began to multiply on the face of the earth, and daughters were born unto them.

> Genesis 6:7—And the Lord said, I will destroy man whom I have created from the face of the earth . . .

> Genesis 6:17—And, behold, I, even I, do bring a flood of waters upon the earth, to destroy all flesh, wherein *is* the breath of life, from under heaven; *and* every thing that is in the earth shall die.

> Genesis 7:4—For yet seven days, and I will cause it to rain upon the earth forty days and forty nights; and every living substance that I have made will I destroy from off the face of the earth.

> Genesis 7:23—And every living substance was destroyed which was upon the face of the ground, both man, and cattle, and the creeping things, and the fowl of the heaven; and they were destroyed from the earth: and Noah only remained *alive,* and they that *were* with him in the ark.

What is the meaning of the repeated phrase "the face of the earth"? There are other verses in the Old Testament that might shed some light on the question. For example, after Cain had killed Abel, his punishment was not death, it was exile. Cain was banished from his homeland to become a fugitive. It seems to be a pretty light sentence, but still Cain complained to the Lord about his punishment.

> Behold, thou hast driven me out this day from the face of the earth; and from thy face shall I be hid; and I shall be a fugitive and a vagabond in the earth; and it shall come to pass, that every one that findeth me shall slay me. (Genesis 4:14)

If "the face of the earth" meant the entire surface of our planet, Cain was going to have to figure out how to levitate to be driven off of it. Only if this phrase means "the local region," does this verse make any sense. Cain was exiled and he had to leave his home, which to him was the face of the earth.

If you run a search of "the face of the earth" in your electronic scriptures, you will find other verses in which the phrase is used (Genesis 11:8, Genesis 41:56, Exodus 10:5 & 15, Exodus 33:16). But in each case, the interpretation of the phrase to mean "the region roundabout" makes more sense than "the entire world." Granted, even in Noah's day, the size of the "face of the earth" may have included several hundred square miles. But since the New World was not yet discovered, it is very unlikely the Old Testament authors would have ever referenced it. Thus, the scriptures do not ever state that Noah's flood was a global flood. In fact, a regional flood actually is much easier to defend. Interpreting the flood as being global is a tradition that has grown over the centuries without any real scriptural basis.

IMPLICATIONS OF A NON-GLOBAL FLOOD

One of the points made in earlier chapters discussing the Creation was that God uses natural means to accomplish His goals. When God does not need to use miracles, He doesn't. Accepting that Noah's flood was regional and not global makes Noah's Ark much simpler and greatly reduces the required magnitude of miracles.

First, there is plenty of water in the world for a regional flood. As everyone knows, regional floods are really quite common. There have been a number of proposals as to where Noah's Flood might have occurred. One proposal is that the flood occurred when the rising Mediterranean Sea broke through a land bridge and flooded into what is now the Black Sea.[5] Secondly, if only Adam's direct descendants living in the region around Noah's village were drowned, the many races of men (Asian, African, Eskimo, pygmies, Nordic, etc.) would not have had to descend from Noah's family in just a few thousand years. Finally, if the flood was regional and not global, Noah would not have had to bring two of every species *from everywhere in the world* upon the ark. Granted, the flooding of that large area of Mesopotamia would have had a devastating effect on the wildlife in the region. But, if the flood was confined to a given region, then after the flood waters receded, the wildlife in the sur-rounding areas could have gradually repopulated the flood plain on its own accord. There would have been no need for Noah to have gathered, housed, and fed the wild animals, untamed birds, snakes, rats, and other creeping things for months. All Noah would really have had to save were his domesticated cattle, sheep, fowls and other farm animals. The only food he would have had to collect would have been food for his family and feed for his livestock.

There is a picture in most LDS chapel libraries that show two of every species, including giraffes and zebras, filing two-by-two into a huge ark. But there is no scriptural proof of the validity of such an image. The scriptures actually state,

> And of every living thing of all flesh, two of every *sort* shalt thou bring into the ark, to keep *them* alive with thee; they shall be male and female.
> Of fowls after their kind, and of cattle after their kind, of every creeping thing of the earth after his kind, two of every *sort* shall come unto thee, to keep *them* alive. (Genesis 6:19–20)

There is no listing of exotic animals coming in from distant lands, an occurrence that surely would have been noteworthy in such an account. These verses list only three types of animals—fowls, cattle, and creeping things. Of the fowls, it appears that Noah had a raven and some doves. But it seems likely he took chickens and related fowls for food. The word "cattle" can mean sheep, cows, goats, and other farm animals (see Genesis 30:32 and its footnote). Both fowls and cattle are common farm animals. Though at the mention of "creeping things" we tend to think of insects, the expression can also mean rabbits and other small but edible animals. The point is that Noah probably did not have to take along any species that he and his family could not have used for survival after the flood.

In regard to the number of each species Noah was to take, the first verses of Genesis chapter 7 actually disagree with chapter 6. Thus, some believe that these verses may have been added later. In any case, these verses slant even more toward a preference for edible, or "clean" animals under the future Mosaic law.

> Of every clean beast thou shalt take to thee by sevens, the male and his female: and of beasts that *are* not clean by two, the male and his female.
>
> Of fowls also of the air by sevens, the male and the female; to keep seed alive upon the face of all the earth. (Genesis 7:2–3)

So, there is very little in the scriptures to support the idea of a global flood and of an ark that saved every species of animal that lived on the earth at that time. There is every indication that Noah was a righteous man who was warned of a coming regional flood and was told to build an ark to save his family and the stock animals needed to support and reestablish their way of life after the flood had receded. Does such an interpretation really take anything away from the story of Noah's Ark? Doesn't it teach the same lesson without global destruction? Not only is such an interpretation easier to believe, it is easier to reconcile with our perception of God. It seemed that a cleansing of the people in a small region of the world at the time had to occur. Did that need also require that millions of animals, most of them living thousands of miles away, had to die as well? As discussed previously, though it is believed there were many other people in the world besides Adam, they were not "Man" and were not part of the Creation story. God was only angry with Adam's posterity because only the children of Adam had received the teachings and commandments from God—and then rejected them. It was they who were disobeying those commandments and it was only they who deserved the punishment. Why would God have wiped out every living person and creature on the entire earth to punish a relatively few men? A regional flood avoids the problems of a very excessive punishment of innocents and the accusation that God would destroy a whole planet for the sins of a few people. Thus geology can lead us to a better, more accurate understanding of the scriptures.

Notes

1. David Montgomery, *The Rocks Don't Lie* (New York: W. W. Norton, 2012), xii.
2. Edward Stillingfleet, *Sacred Origins*.
3. Athanasius Kircher, *Arca Noe* (1675).
4. Colin McEvedy and Richard Jones, *Atlas of World Population History* (New York: Facts on File, 1979), 344.
5. Ian Wilson, *Before the Flood* (New York: St. Martin's Press, 2001).
6. Montgomery, *The Rocks Don't Lie*, 43.

11

AUTHORSHIP OF
THE SCRIPTURES

S o far, we have come to see how advances in astronomy, biology, genetics, and paleontology have led us to new understandings of the scriptural account of the Creation. Geological discoveries have led to new conclusions regarding Noah's Flood. No longer at odds with the continued revelations of science, our mental testimonies can grow stronger.

The scriptures are a foundation of all Christian religions. As we have seen, the findings of science have forced us to reinterpret accounts we find there—such as the narratives of the Creation and Noah's Ark. But the history and authorship of the scriptures themselves have been called into question for years. Were the "Books of Moses" (the first five books of the Bible) actually written by Moses? Did Joshua write the book of Joshua and Ruth the book of Ruth? Are we secure in our knowledge about the authorship of the books of the New Testament?

There is a whole science that has arisen to answer such questions. That science is, rather unfortunately termed Higher Criticism. Though it sounds like these biblical scholars are arrogant critics of the Bible, they are not. Higher Criticism is the study of the historic origins, literary structure, authorship, and dating of the books of the Bible, especially the Old Testament. So how does one establish the publication date of the ancient books of the Bible? You compare it to other ancient writings whose publication dates are known. You compare the wording, syntax, phrases, names, and expressions of the undated manuscripts to the wording of dated writings and thus approximate the date when the book was probably written.

For example, if you were reading a book with no title page or publication date, you could probably get an idea of when it was written by the wording used in the book. For example, if the author describes something he considers especially impressive, whether he used the word "wonderful," "keen," "neato," "the bee's knees," "rad," "groovy," "far out," "cool," "sick," or "awesome" would tell you something about the author and the decade in which he lived. Both words and how they are structured into sentences change with time. You could certainly identify Shakespeare from more modern authors by his use of Early Modern English sentence structure. Finally, names will tell you something about the time period of a particular writing. The Soviet Union dissolved in 1991 so any references to it as a country in the present tense (i.e., other than as historical notes) would place the writing before that year.

Biblical scholars use the same methods. Experts in ancient Samarian and Hebrew apply their knowledge of grammar, syntax, names, dialects, jargon, and commonly-used phrases to determine when and where an ancient writing took place. Languages change and ninth-century Hebrew is different from fifth-century Hebrew. Study of the writings by cultures surrounding ancient Israel also sheds light on scriptural interpretation. Such studies by Biblical scholars may require some readjustments to our perceptions of the Bible. But, in doing so, it will also help us understand those scriptures better. This is the essence of developing a mental testimony. Errors and misinterpretations in the Bible should not surprise Latter-day Saints. We have been taught of their existence for years.

THE BIBLE

For centuries, the Bible has been considered by the Christian world to be the Word of God. Thus, the Bible has been held with the utmost reverence. During the middle ages, entire monasteries devoted their time and resources to copying the Bible with beautiful script and illustrations. Today, many Christians still consider the Bible to be a perfect book and that each and every word comes directly from God. For these people, any criticism of the Bible is blasphemous. However, as members of the LDS Church, we do not believe the Bible to be a perfect book. Our eighth article of faith states that "We believe the Bible to be the word of God as far as it is translated correctly." Statements by Joseph Smith indicate he may have been surprised at the number of errors he found in the Bible.

> I believe the Bible as it read when it came from the pen of the original writers. Ignorant translators, careless transcribers, or designing and corrupt priests have committed many errors.
>
> There are many things in the Bible which do not, as they now stand, accord with the revelations of the Holy Ghost to me.[1]

In his desire to help other members to better understand the concepts taught in the scriptures, Joseph Smith spent many hours in study and prayer trying to make corrections to it. Many of these corrections can be found as footnotes in the LDS-published Bible. Where there are so many corrections that footnotes become burdensome, there is a section included in the LDS-published Bible to hold them all. Corrections are made from Genesis 1 to Revelations. One Old Testament book is thrown out altogether. Under its entry in the Bible Dictionary, it is pointed out that the prophet Joseph stated that, "The Song of Solomon is not inspired scripture."[2] The same Bible Dictionary source states that "whether Solomon is actually the author is doubtful."

Just like the authorship of the Song of Solomon is questioned, so too is the authorship of many other books of the Bible. In the next pages, we are going to find that our perception of the accuracy of the Scriptures may require some adjustment. In doing so, we need to understand that we can have faith in what the scriptures teach while understanding that the scriptures themselves are not perfect. Scholars have brought much of the Bible under question. Those who study the scriptures should be aware of the research, keeping in mind that questioning the authorship of the scriptures is not the same thing as questioning its precepts.

THE AUTHORSHIP OF
THE PENTATEUCH

For centuries, the Christian and Judaic worlds have believed that Moses wrote the Pentateuch, or the first five books of the Old Testament. It makes sense after all. Moses's birth is recorded in the second chapter of Exodus and he dies in the last chapter of Deuteronomy, so his life is nicely bracketed by these four books. Given that these four books contain the very detailed specifics of the Mosaic law, it seemed a pretty safe conclusion that Moses was involved in their writing.

But there are many Biblical scholars who believe that Moses's writings were significantly edited between the scrolls he inked and the books we read today. There is good evidence for such doubt. For example, in all these books, Moses is always referred to in the third person. The writer never uses "I" when describing Moses, which Moses might naturally have done if he were the writer. Numbers 12:3 reads, "Now the man Moses was very meek, above all the men which were upon the earth." It is unlikely that Moses would have said this about himself, especially if he really was the meekest man on earth. Finally, Moses dies in Deuteronomy 34:5, is buried in the next verse, and his 30 days of mourning is reported a couple of verses later. Moses could not have written these words himself of course. But we read of no passing off from Moses to another author at this point; in fact, there is no interruption to the narrative at all. While these questions were a little bothersome, there were more serious clues that something was amiss that led to questions of who wrote the Pentateuch.

One of the reasons the Old Testament can be hard to read is the presence of so many doublets. As defined by Richard Friedman in his book *Who Wrote the Bible?*

> A doublet is a case of the same story being told twice. Even in translation it is easy to observe that biblical stories often appear with variations of detail in two different places in the Bible. There are two different stories of the creation of the world. There are two stories of the covenant between God and the patriarch Abraham, two stories of the naming of Abraham's son Isaac, two stories of Abraham's claiming to a foreign king that his wife Sarah is his sister, two stories of Isaac's son Jacob making a journey to Mesopotamia, two stories of

a revelation to Jacob in Beth-El, two stories of God's changing Jacob's name to Israel, two stories of Moses' getting water from a rock at a place called Meribah, and more.[3]

The most logical explanation for doublets is that two different accounts of the same biblical event were written by two different authors and preserved by ancient Jewish priests. Later Jewish scriptorians, aghast at the thought of deleting any words of the Bible, included both of the accounts in their translations. Sometimes the second account of the doublet is in a completely different chapter. Sometimes it has been weaved into the first account, making the reading somewhat confusing. Biblical scholars, noting the two story lines present in such weavings, began the process of untangling the two accounts. This research is not a recent occurrence. The discovery of doublets and their untangling was first published by three separate men in the 1700s.[4] By 1800, biblical scholars recognized that there were not just two separate accounts combined to form the Pentateuch, there were at least four! The theory that the first five books of the Old Testament were written by numerous writers was eventually dubbed "The Documentary Hypothesis."

The first doublet in the Bible describes the Creation. Genesis chapter 1 gives its version of the Creation. Genesis 2 gives a second version, filling in some of the gaps omitted in chapter 1, such as the name of the garden, that Adam was created from the dust, that Adam named the animals, and that Eve was created from one of Adam's ribs. One explanation for this redundancy is that Genesis 2 includes verses that pertain to the spiritual creation. This may be true, but having the spiritual creation in chapter 2 rather emphasizes the problem. Why do the books read so similarly and why did the author recount the Creation narrative in reverse chronological order? Though our English translation of Genesis masks it a bit, the names for God are different in each of these two chapters. In Genesis 1, the author refers to the Creator only as Elohim, translated as "God" in the King James Version no fewer than 35 times. In chapter 2, the author refers to the creator as Yahweh Elohim, translated "Lord God" and not simply Elohim. There is no indication that God's name or title changed between the two chapters. It appears to be simply that two different authors had different preferred names for God.

There are two excellent books written about the Documentary Hypothesis. The first, already referenced above, is *Who Wrote the Bible?* by Richard Friedman. The second is *Authoring the Old Testament* by LDS author David Bokovoy.[5] In both of those texts you can find the disentangled stories of the second major doublet in the scriptures: Noah's Ark. Though details vary a little, when separated out each of the doublets reads quite well and it becomes apparent that these really were two stories woven into one. Another doublet is found in the story of Joseph being captured by his brothers, cast into a pit, and then sold to slave traders making their way to Egypt. Again, the separated accounts each make more sense than the combined doublet account of Genesis 37.

If many of the Old Testament stories were recounted by more than one person, who were those multiple authors? The Documentary Hypothesis proposes that there were four main authors of the Pentateuch, identified by the letters J, E, P, and D. The writings of these authors were separated out using their jargon, word patterns, etc. In doing so, the beliefs, prejudices, and biases of these four men began to make themselves apparent from the wording they used. From those biases and an understanding of the history of Israel and Judah, enough evidence was collected to propose who these men were, where they lived, and when they wrote their versions of scripture. J, E, P, and D could each have been one man, or a group of men. We really cannot know for certain. But, from their words, we can have some insight into their politics, beliefs, and loyalties.

THE DOCUMENTARY HYPOTHESIS

The first author (or group of authors) is identified as "J," because they use the term Jehovah (or Yahweh) when referring to God, as is found in Genesis 2. As David Bokovoy describes this account, "J was likely written by Judean scribes from the Southern kingdom of Judah, as many of the geographical references in its narrative focus upon the Southern Territory."[6] This was the first of the authors who, it is believed, included their edits to the biblical books in about the 7th century BC.

The second author of the four is called "P" and stands for "Priestly" because this author is continually focused on priestly responsibilities such as rituals, sacrifice, dietary laws, temple architecture, genealogies, and purity. P is also concerned with dates, numbers, and measurements. P was written after J, probably in the 6ᵗʰ century BC, but like J, was written by priests of the tribe of Judah. P was very concerned with emphasizing that priest's responsibilities should only be done only by priests. In P's interpretation of Israelite history, the first High Priest was Aaron. Thus, P does not include the story of Cain and Abel, since both offered sacrifices to the Lord, though neither were priests. P also skips the part in the story of Noah's Ark about Noah bringing sacrificial animals onto the Ark and sacrificing them when the flood waters receded. In P's opinion Noah was not a priest either, so should not have been offering sacrifices. Aaron, the first High Priest, is always featured in a positive light in P's writings.[6]

For the first fourteen chapters of Genesis, the Bible switches back and forth between narratives of J and P. Then in Genesis 15, we see text from our third author make an appearance. This contributor is abbreviated E, referring to his practice of always using the name "Elohim" when referring to God. E was unique because he was almost certainly a member of one of the northern tribes of Israel. If you remember from your Old Testament readings, relationships between Israel and Judah were often contentious. Time and again E takes the side of Israel, while J takes the side of Judah. There are numerous examples of this bias, but Dr. Friedman gives us a couple of examples,

> Both J and E have versions of the story of Joseph. In both, Joseph's brothers are jealous of him and plan to kill him, but one of the brothers saves him. In E it is Reuben, the oldest, who saves him. But in J it is *Judah* who saves him.
>
> In E, Moses' faithful assistant is Joshua. Joshua leads the people in battle against the Amalekites . . . he is the only Israelite who is not involved in the golden calf incident and he seeks to prevent the misuse of prophecy. In J, on the other hand, Joshua plays no role. Why the special treatment of Joshua in E but not in J? Joshua was a *northern* hero. [7]

The final author is D, since his writings are wholly contained in Deuteronomy, the final book of the Pentateuch. According to the Bible Dictionary, "The book contains the last discourses of Moses delivered in the plains of Moab just before his death." Much of Deuteronomy is a review of the Mosaic law which we have read before. For example, Deuteronomy 5:6–21 is a nearly word-for-word repetition of the Ten Commandments found in Exodus 20.

From the text of Deuteronomy, scholars have concluded that this book was probably written by a priest from the Northern kingdom of Israel, since, like E, he focuses on issues of the north. D was also probably a Levite priest, possibly from the city of Shiloh. Deuteronomy repeatedly favors the Levites with praise and recognition. It prohibits the people from carrying out their own sacrifices, since that is the responsibility of the Levites. It instructs the people to "do according to all that the priests the Levites shall teach you" (Deuteronomy 24:8, 33:8–11) and to provide for the Levites.

The last character proposed in the Documentary Hypothesis was called the "Redactor," or the ancient Israelite editor who put these four narratives together to give us the final version of the first five books of the Old Testament.

WHAT ABOUT MOSES?

Despite the claims of the Documentary Theory, the title pages of the first five books in my King James Bible declare them to be books of Moses. Both the Book of Mormon (1 Nephi 5:11) and the Pearl of Great Price (Moses 1:40–41) reaffirm that Moses wrote these books as well. But with all the evidence presented in support of the Documentary Theory and the way it explains Biblical redundancies and inconsistencies, can Moses still be the author?

Though we have pointed out the differences between the accounts of the four authors, we also have to recognize the many similarities as well. Reading these different accounts is like listening to witnesses recount the same event, but, due to their own viewpoints and biases, emphasize different aspects of that event. But all four authors had to start with some ancient documents as their source material. It is believed that Moses was born in about 1400 BC. Thus if Moses had written the documents that were used by our J, P, E, and D in 600–700 BC, those manuscripts would have been about 700 years old. So our four authors may have been reading copies of copies of Moses's original writings. The generations of priests who kept these records over those centuries would probably have revered the writings of Moses and most would have done their best to copy them exactly. But, over time, changes were made.

To be fair to J, P, E, and D, they probably wrote their manuscripts with the best of intentions. They could have thought that the old scripts needed to be corrected or updated to reflect the more progressive (and improved) understanding of God's commands. They may have thought they were just clarifying parts of the scriptures with additional explanation and dropping out parts that were misleading. Let's face it, new generations usually think that they are more enlightened than generations of the past.

To understand this attitude, we must consider the audience J, P, E, and D were addressing. To compare, let's look at the four gospels of the New Testament. The book of Matthew was written "to persuade the Jews that Jesus is the promised Messiah."[8] To do so, Matthew points out the Savior's genealogy through David and His fulfillment of several Old Testament prophecies of Christ. Mark, however, writes to a Gentile audience, so he emphasizes the miracles of Christ and gives explanations that would have been unnecessary for a Jewish reader. The book of John is written "to members of the Church who already had basic information about the Lord. His primary purpose was to emphasize the divine nature of Jesus as the Only Begotten Son of God in the flesh."[8] In other words, Matthew, Mark, and John all had their own agendas as they wrote the books that we venerate today as scripture. Each writer had a similar goal in mind as he wrote—to convince one particular group of people that Jesus of Nazareth was the Son of God. But each audience needed to read different words to be persuaded.

The four Documentary Hypothesis authors J, P, E, and D also had their agendas. As priests they knew they were writing not only to their own people but to future generations of Israel and Judah. Thus, these men (and undoubtedly others over the centuries) were able to justify the edits they made to the original writings of Moses. While it was important to preserve history, they must have thought it was just as important to preserve what they believed to be correct doctrine.

WHO WROTE THE OTHER
OLD TESTAMENT BOOKS?

After Deuteronomy, most of the rest of the Old Testament books are titled with a personal name, such as Joshua, Ruth, and Samuel. Generally, we tend to think that those books were written by that person. So we believe that Joshua wrote the Book of Joshua, Ruth wrote the book of Ruth and so on, throughout the both the Old and New Testaments. In many of these books, there is actual evidence that this is true and the names are justified. But if such evidence is not present, we should recognize that it is often only oral tradition that declares the authors of these books.

For example, we don't know who wrote the book of Ruth, though few scriptorians believe that it was Ruth herself. The author of Ecclesiastes claims to be Solomon, but the writing style is that of someone who lived 600 years after his death. The book of Daniel was believed to be written by Daniel while he was being held captive in Babylon in 600 BC. But scholars date the writing style and wording at 400 years later.[9] Tradition has taught that the prophet Samuel wrote the book of Samuel, though he is not born until 20 verses into the account. Thus it appears that many of the books of the Old Testament were either written or revised at later dates than when the stories unfolded.

In AD 393–397, the learned men of the Catholic Church met in formal councils to determine which of the books that were being studied in the churches at that time should be canonized. There were some books being studied that were not in the Hebrew Bible but had been included in its Greek version (the Septuagint). These books were of doubtful authorship and origin, but contained teachings that some considered to be valuable. In the end, the Catholic Church canonized these books. Now called the Apocrypha, they are still part of the Catholic scriptures today. The Protestant religions, on the other hand, were more dubious. They did not canonize the Apocryphal writings though earlier Protestant Bibles did include them in a separate section of the book.

When Joseph Smith was translating the Bible to remove errors and make corrections, he asked the Lord if he should work on the Apocrypha as well. In Doctrine and Covenants chapter 91, he was given the answer. He was told, "There are many things contained therein that are true, and it is mostly translated correctly; There are many things contained therein that are not true, which are interpolations by the hands of men" (D&C 91:2). "Interpolations" are entries in a text that were not written by the author, but are included at a later time by others. The Lord was recognizing that there were errors and additions to these books, which took away from truth of those writings. He told Joseph not to translate them. But then He goes on to say, "And whoso is enlightened by the Spirit shall obtain benefit therefrom." The point is that, even when reading teachings that admittedly have some errors and additions, we can obtain benefit from reading them. Our Bible may have doublets, insertions, and edits by scribes who thought they were improving the original manuscripts. But it is still scripture and we will benefit from its reading.

AUTHORSHIP OF NEW TESTAMENT BOOKS

The earliest days of the Church of Jesus Christ following the Savior's death were very turbulent and chaotic. The church was growing rapidly. But travel was very slow, and the Apostles and other church leadership were hard-pressed to keep in contact with the members of their far-flung congregations. Persecution by Jewish and Roman enemies was ongoing. Peter and John were arrested and questioned (Acts 4:3). Stephen was stoned to death (Acts 7:59–60) and James was killed by Herod (Acts 12:2). Peter had received the revelation that the gospel should be preached to the Gentiles, greatly expanding the potential mission field. The doctrine of the church on many issues was still being established. We don't know what the apostles were teaching verbally, but major doctrines of the early church such as circumcision (Galatians 5:6), eating sacrificed meat (Corinthians 8), and resurrection (1 Corinthians 15:12) were still being explained by Paul in his letters long after he had helped found the congregations. Given the diversity within the church (Jews, Gentiles, Romans, Greeks, etc.), there was great dispute regarding the true doctrine of the church.

Since travel was so long and difficult, the Apostles often chose to write letters to the more distant congregations of the church (Acts 15:23). These letters were reverenced and accepted by congregations as doctrine.

In this environment, it is believed that some Christians, disagreeing with certain doctrines being taught in their church, decided to influence that doctrine. They turned to forgery. Knowing that a letter signed by an apostle would certainly cause the congregation to modify a particular doctrine within their congregation, it would have been fairly easy to write a letter and sign Paul's name to it. As explained by Hugh Nibley,

> These people made a practice of claiming to be the unique and secret possessors of the earliest Christian writings. To make good their claims, they did not hesitate to practice forgery, and they borrowed freely from any available source.[10]

Dr. Nibley goes on to explain that some of those available sources were genuine old Christian writings, so some of these forgeries preserved a good deal of valuable material. Early Christian communities accepted many letters and epistles as doctrines that are not in our New Testament today. These letters were studied in church services, along with the Old Testament writings they had available. This went on for many years, until the Catholic Church decided it was time to canonize the books they believed to be genuine apostolic writings and rid themselves of the forgeries. As described by Lenet Hadley Read,

> By the fourth century precisely what was "official scripture" was finally decided. Athanasius (A.D. 293–373), the bishop of Alexandria, publicly listed as authoritative scripture the same twenty-seven books we have in our present New Testament. Some books whose authority scholars like Origen had questioned were included on this list— among them the books of James, Hebrews, 2 Peter, and 2 and 3 John. Other books that had been held dear by some early Christians, were not on the list.[11]

Athanasius's chosen books were accepted as canon by the Catholic Church in councils held in Laodicea, Hippo, and Carthage. As mentioned earlier, these councils also debated which Old Testament writings should be canonized as well.

Please note that these decisions occurred in 300 AD, over 1,700 years ago. We have come a long way since then. Linguists and scriptorians have analyzed the books of the New Testament word by word, using computers to search for writing styles and patterns. This in-depth research has uncovered new findings regarding authorship and the probable time period of those writings. New conclusions were inevitable.

According to his book *Forged,* Bart Ehrman argued that the three books of the New Testament called the Pastoral Epistles—1 Timothy, 2 Timothy, and Titus—were the first books that were called out as possible forgeries.[12] In 1807, a German scholar named Friedrich Schleiermacher published a letter that argued that 1 Timothy used words and ideas that were at odds with those in the other letters of Paul. The Pastoral Epistles address church organization, such as qualifications for bishops and deacons, before any such organizations were in place. These books address false teachings such as "the resurrection is past already" (2 Timothy 2:18), expectations of church leadership, and the role of women in the church. These were issues that the church faced in the second century, not in Paul's time.

It is also believed that verses have been added to some of Paul's original letters. In 1 Corinthians 14:34–35, we read a scathing rebuke of women in the church. Women were to be silent in church and submissive to their husbands. In the verses before and after these two verses, Paul is teaching about prophecy in the church. Verses 34 and 35 simply don't fit and it is believed they were added into the middle of Paul's letter at a later date. If 1 Timothy is also a forgery, it removes the second rebuke of women in the New Testament found in 1 Timothy 2:11–15. Again, in these verses women are told to be silent with all subjection, but that they can be saved by childbearing. From these verses it has been believed for centuries that Paul was an incurable male chauvinist. If these verses are forgeries of Paul's writings, it vindicates Paul from an unfair conclusion.

There are some doubts about others of Paul's books in the New Testament as well, including 2 Thessalonians, Ephesians, and Colossians. The sure identification of forgeries is difficult in that only parts of those letters may have been forged, as was illustrated with 1 Corinthians. Besides Paul's letters, at least one letter thought to be written by Peter was also probably forged.[13]

Though we believe that our scriptures contain the teachings of the prophets, there is evidence that they may not contain their exact wording of their original texts. But this possibility should not shake our mental testimonies. We already believe the Bible to be the word of God *as far as it is translated correctly*, a condition that Joseph Smith obviously wanted to emphasize so much that he included it in our eighth article of faith. We still understand that there are correct principles taught in the Bible, whether they are taught by known or unknown authors. This knowledge helps us recognize the few untrue principles (such as that women are to remain silent in church) have crept into our scriptures. We can still have faith in the Bible, though we understand in our minds that some of the assumptions made about the authorship of the Bible may be incorrect. We have never believed that the Bible is a perfect book. The realization that there are errors and unknown authorships in the Bible simply illustrates the need for continuing latter-day revelation.

NOTES

1. *Discourses of the Prophet Joseph Smith*, 245.
2. LDS Bible Dictionary "Song of Solomon," 776.
3. Richard Friedman, *Who Wrote the Bible?* (New York: Harper Collins, 1987), 22.
4. Ibid., 52.
5. David Bokovoy, *Authoring the Old Testament* (Salt Lake City, UT: Greg Kofford, 2014).
6. Ibid., 43, 51.
7. Friedman, *Who Wrote the Bible?*, 65–66.
8. LDS Bible Dictionary, "Gospels," 682–683.
9. Bart Ehrman, *Forged* (New York: Harper Collins, 2011).
10. Hugh Nibley, *Since Cumorah* (Salt Lake City: Deseret Book, 1967), 85.
11. Lenet Hadley Read, *How We Got the Bible* (Salt Lake City: Deseret Book, 1985), 41.
12. Ehrman, *Forged*.
13. Ibid., 68.

12

THE WORD OF WISDOM DIET

There is science and then there is pseudoscience. Pseudoscience is defined as "A system of theories or assertions about the natural world that claim or appear to be scientific but that, in fact, are not."[1] In no area of science is there more of a problem with pseudoscience than in food.

As a people, we love food. The taste of a well-prepared meal, or a well-prepared dessert, is one of the major joys of life. In fact, we apparently love food too much. We are eating too much and, thus, obesity levels throughout the world are at an all-time high. Our doctors tell us that obesity is a health risk and that we should exercise and eat less. But hunger is first distracting and then painful, so dieting is not fun. Thus many people have looked for new diets that will make weight loss easier. Entire industries have been created to meet the desire for weight loss and maintaining a healthy, attractive body. Many companies continue to develop new products or diets they can market to this large customer base. Billions of dollars are at stake, so it is not surprising that the food industry is rife with pseudoscience. Navigating through all the claims and marketing to find the real truth about what we should eat is a challenge, but we do find the basics for a good diet in our scriptures.

THE WORD OF
WISDOM DIET

We have received revelation regarding what we should and should not eat. It is well known that faithful Mormons do not drink alcohol (D&C 89:5–7), do not smoke or otherwise use tobacco (D&C 89:6), and do not drink coffee and tea (D&C 89:9). These prohibitions make up a part of a commandment that we call the Word of Wisdom. We could review all of the studies that have been done to show the prophetic truthfulness of the Word of Wisdom, but that has been done before. Tobacco products do cause cancer, alcohol in excess is harmful, and coffee and tea can be hard on the stomach. As a people, we felt vindicated as the medical sciences eventually demonstrated that the Word of Wisdom revelation was correct in its recommendations.

But then the revelation goes on to give us advice as to what we *should* consume. This is the part of the Word of Wisdom that is rarely considered in any detail. For example, in interviews for temple recommends, our Church leader will always ask members if they are avoiding alcohol, tobacco, coffee, and tea. He will rarely ask members if they are eating healthy, which is what the latter half of the revelation discusses. This is understandable, since it is very difficult to define "eating healthy." But if we really believe our body is a temple (1 Corinthians 6:19), then we should be equally as concerned about what goes into it as what stays out.

This part of the Word of Wisdom revelation reads,

> And again, verily I say unto you, all wholesome herbs God hath ordained for the constitution, nature, and use of man—
>
> Every herb in the season thereof, and every fruit in the season thereof; all these to be used with prudence and thanksgiving.
>
> Yea, flesh also of beasts and of the fowls of the air, I, the Lord, have ordained for the use of man with thanksgiving; nevertheless they are to be used sparingly;
>
> And it is pleasing unto me that they should not be used, only in times of winter, or of cold, or famine.
>
> All grain is ordained for the use of man and of beasts, to be the staff of life, not only for man but for the beasts of the field, and the fowls of heaven, and all wild animals that run or creep on the earth;
>
> And these hath God made for the use of man only in times of famine and excess of hunger.

All grain is good for the food of man; as also the fruit of the vine;
that which yieldeth fruit, whether in the ground or above the ground.
(D&C 89:10–16)

This is very specific advice, from which we can summarize the basics
of a healthy diet. Diets are a big business after all. Hundreds of diet books
have been published in the past few decades. So, in the following pages, let
us determine the Word of Wisdom diet and compare it to the recommendations of the United States government. The United States Department of
Agriculture (USDA) has a website called Choose My Plate, which replaced
the food pyramid that had been used for years. At this site, the USDA
reveals its recommendations on what we should eat to have a healthy diet,
based on decades of nutritional studies. The following summaries are
taken almost directly from the Choose My Plate website.[2]

FRUITS AND VEGETABLES—
WORD OF WISDOM

First, wholesome herbs are recommended. These include the normal
herbs with which we are familiar (e.g., basil, thyme, cilantro, dill,
fennel, garlic, and mint). But it is doubtful the Lord would have first
recognized food ingredients added only for taste and not nutrition in
this important revelation. As it turns out, the word "herbs" was used
to describe foods that we would recognize as vegetables today. As one
curator of historic landscapes explained, "For the first immigrants—
the colonists—who came here in the 17th century, every plant around
them was an herb. The term vegetable didn't even come into common
use until the 18th century."[3] The Lord is actually recommending vegetables as well as the normal taste-enhancing herbs we more commonly
define as herbs today.

Right after vegetables, the Lord recommends the consumption of
fruit. Then He sets two conditions of eating vegetables and fruits. First,
He states that we are to eat, "Every herb in the season thereof, and every
fruit in the season thereof." The second condition is the command that
"all these to be used with prudence and thanksgiving." This command
of moderation and appreciation in regard to food is actually repeated
several times in the scriptures.

FRUITS AND VEGETABLES— USDA RECOMMENDATIONS

Now let us compare our scriptural recommendations with those of our own USDA.

> Fruits and vegetables provide nutrients vital for health and maintenance of your body. Most whole fruits and vegetables are naturally low in fat, sodium, and calories. None have cholesterol. Fruits and vegetables are important sources of many nutrients, including potassium, dietary fiber, folate (folic acid), vitamin A, and vitamin C. Eating a diet rich in vegetables and fruits as part of an overall healthy diet may reduce risk for heart disease, including heart attack and stroke. A diet rich in a variety of whole fruits and vegetables may protect against certain types of cancers and can reduce the risk of heart disease, obesity, and type 2 diabetes. Eating vegetables and fruits rich in potassium may lower blood pressure, reduce the risk of developing kidney stones, and help decrease bone loss. Being lower in calories, vegetables and some whole fruits can help lower calorie intake.[2]

MEATS—WORD OF WISDOM

In Doctrine and Covenants 89:12, almost as if He is clarifying a point of debate among his people, the Lord points out that we do not have to be vegetarians—we are allowed to eat meat: "Yea, flesh also of beasts and of the fowls of the air, I, the Lord, have ordained for the use of man with thanksgiving." So, we are allowed to eat meat, but the Lord then adds the proviso, "nevertheless they are to be used sparingly." In the next verse, He repeats Himself by adding, "It is pleasing unto me that they should not be used, only in times of winter, or of cold, or famine." Please note that this part of the revelation is a bit confusing due to the wording used in the early 1800s. The Lord is not saying that meats should not be eaten, as the first part of the sentence implies. He is recommending that meats be eaten sparingly. In times of winter, cold, or famine, the Lord recognizes that we will often need to eat more meat than normal since, in the early days of the Church, fruits and vegetables were not as available in those seasons. In times of a bountiful harvest, our meat consumption can and should be less.

The Lord repeats this directive in several scriptures. He assures us that the beasts of the field and the fowls of the air are ordained for the use of man. He offers us the fullness of the earth. But He apparently still has some concern for those beasts and fowl, for He forbids the wasting of flesh and commands that we use good judgement, with dire consequences if we don't.

> And whoso forbiddeth to abstain from meats, that man should not eat the same, is not ordained of God;
>
> For, behold, the beasts of the field and the fowls of the air, and that which cometh of the earth, is ordained for the use of man for food and for raiment, and that he might have in abundance.
>
> But it is not given that one man should possess that which is above another, wherefore the world lieth in sin.
>
> And wo be unto man that sheddeth blood or that wasteth flesh and hath no need. (D&C 49:18–21)

> Verily I say, that inasmuch as ye do this, the fulness of the earth is yours, the beasts of the field and the fowls of the air, and that which climbeth upon the trees and walketh upon the earth;
>
> Yea, and the herb, and the good things which come of the earth, whether for food or for raiment, or for houses, or for barns, or for orchards, or for gardens, or for vineyards;
>
> Yea, all things which come of the earth, in the season thereof, are made for the benefit and the use of man, both to please the eye and to gladden the heart;
>
> Yea, for food and for raiment, for taste and for smell, to strengthen the body and to enliven the soul.
>
> And it pleaseth God that he hath given all these things unto man; for unto this end were they made to be used, with judgment, not to excess, neither by extortion. (D&C 59:16–20)

Notably, in other scriptures, the Lord routinely differentiates between the three types of animals that He has created; beasts, fowls of the air, and fishes (Genesis 1:26–28, Zephaniah 1:3, D&C 117:6, D&C 29:24, D&C 101:24, Abraham 4:26, 28, Moses 2:26, 28). This fact is laid out plainly in 1 Corinthians 15:39, "All flesh is not the same flesh: but there is one kind of flesh of men, another flesh of beasts, another of fishes, and another of birds."

Interestingly, the Lord only mentions the beasts and fowls of the air in regard to His limitation on the amount of meat we should consume.

Fish is not mentioned in His restriction. Though undoubtedly the recommendation of prudence still stands, it appears that fish can make up a large portion of our protein requirements. From this omission, one might conclude that the Lord considers fish to be a more healthy flesh for us to eat.

MEATS—USDA RECOMMENDATIONS

Nutritionists, and thus the USDA, agree with the Lord's assessment of meat. Unlike the recommendations for fruits, vegetables, and grains, the description of the protein foods group (meats) on the USDA website starts with a warning.

> Diets that are high in saturated fats raise "bad" cholesterol levels in the blood. The "bad" cholesterol is called LDL (low-density lipoprotein) cholesterol. High LDL cholesterol, in turn, increases the risk for coronary heart disease. Some food choices in this group are high in saturated fat. These include fatty cuts of beef, pork, and lamb; regular (75% to 85% lean) ground beef; regular sausages, hot dogs, and bacon; some luncheon meats such as regular bologna and salami; and some poultry such as duck. To help keep blood cholesterol levels healthy, limit the amount of these foods you eat. A high intake of fats makes it difficult to avoid consuming more calories than are needed.[2]

SEAFOOD

Fish is the only meat that is not restricted by the Word of Wisdom. Nothing at all is really said about fish and other seafood. Given where He lived, the past occupation of several of His apostles, and the miracle of feeding the 5,000 (Luke 6:38–43), it is pretty certain the Savior ate a good deal of fish. In any case, unlike the other meats, the Word of Wisdom offers no restriction on the amount of fish that we eat. Once again, the USDA website agrees with this recommendation. Fish is high in polyunsaturated fats and is much healthier for you than the saturated fats found in beef and pork.

> Seafood contains a range of nutrients, notably the omega-3 fatty acids, EPA and DHA. Eating about 8 ounces per week of a variety of

seafood contributes to the prevention of heart disease. These include protein, B vitamins (niacin, thiamin, riboflavin, and B6), vitamin E, iron, zinc, and magnesium.[2]

GRAINS—WORD OF WISDOM

The Lord then moves on to recommend grains as a main part of our diets.

All grain is ordained for the use of man and of beasts, to be the staff of life, not only for man but for the beasts of the field, and the fowls of heaven, and all wild animals that run or creep on the earth. (D&C 89:14)

Grain has always been recognized as the "staff of life," not only for man but for the beasts of the field. The Lord then summarizes that,

All grain is good for the food of man; as also the fruit of the vine; that which yieldeth fruit, whether in the ground or above the ground. (D&C 89:16)

This verse approves the consumption of potatoes, beets, and other foods that are grown underground rather than above it. In Doctrine and Covenants 89:17, it seems the Lord spends a verse detailing which grains are best for specific farm animals to illustrate that grains are to be used to feed beasts as well as men. Then, in verses 18–20, we are given this promise:

And all saints who remember to keep and do these sayings, walking in obedience to the commandments, shall receive health in the navel and marrow to their bones; And shall find wisdom and great treasures of knowledge, even hidden treasures; And shall run and not be weary, and shall walk and not faint.

GRAINS—USDA RECOMMENDATIONS

Yet again the USDA agrees with the Word of Wisdom diet.

Eating grains, especially whole grains, provides health benefits. People who eat whole grains as part of a healthy diet have a reduced risk of some chronic diseases. Grains are important sources of many nutrients, including dietary fiber, several B vitamins (thiamin, riboflavin, niacin, and folate), and minerals (iron, magnesium, and selenium). Consuming whole grains as part of a healthy diet may reduce the risk of heart disease. Consuming higher-fiber foods, such as whole grains, as part of a healthy diet, may reduce constipation. Eating whole grains may help with weight management.[2]

Both the USDA and the Word of Wisdom agree that a complete, well-rounded diet of fruits, vegetables, grains, limited meats, and fish is recommended for our daily food. As summarized by the *Dietary* Supplement Health and Education Act (DSCHEA) of 1994, "clinical research has shown that several chronic diseases can be prevented simply with a healthful diet, such as a diet that is low in fat, saturated fat, cholesterol, and sodium, with a high proportion of plant-based foods."[4] This is exactly what the Word of Wisdom recommends as well. Unfortunately, a large number of people are not taking this advice seriously and are being swayed by food pseudoscience that surrounds us.

FAD DIETS

Of all the products and lifestyles available to the public, diets come and go so often that the phrase "fad diets" has become common. We have seen a number of low carbohydrate (low-carb) diets which promote the consumption of an abundance of protein and little to no carbohydrates. There are throw-back diets that hearken back to diets of earlier days. Thus we have new ancient grains products and the paleo diet that recommends we eat the same foods that were eaten by our prehistoric ancestors. A number of diets have been proposed that promote the consumption of one single food. The age-old grapefruit diet, for example, encourages you to eat grapefruit with every meal, but curtail everything else. If you like grapefruit, this diet would sound attractive at first. Of course, after a few days, you get sick of grapefruit and stop eating it. Similar diets include the cabbage soup diet, body cleansing and detoxifying diets, and the so-called "superfoods" (e.g., acai, quinoa, kale, and Greek yogurt) that have their moments of fame and then rejoin the ranks of normal food.

There are diets that encourage you to overconsume water or to drink only ionized and/or alkaline water. There are diets that encourage over-dosing of vitamins A or B or C or D. There are diets that encourage you not to eat any wheat flour products.[5,6] Some diets compare white sugar to poison[7] so forbid it and all other sugar-based sweeteners. There has been a great deal of confusion by the public in regard to healthy diets versus diets that are structured because of allergies. A gluten-free diet is recommended if you are sensitive to gluten and it is highly recommended if you are allergic to gluten (i.e., you have Celiac disease). Likewise, a soy-free diet is recommended if you are allergic to soy and a dairy-free diet if you are allergic to milk proteins. Since nut allergies trigger the most severe, life-threatening reactions, a nut-free diet is *highly* recommended if you are allergic to nuts. But if you are not allergic to these foods, there is no reason to remove them from your diet. Gluten-free diets are especially popular now. Grocery stores have gluten-free areas and restaurants have gluten-free selections on their menus. Oat-based breakfast cereals, popcorn, and many other foods that have *always* been gluten-free are now marketing the fact on their packaging. Thus, many people who strive for healthy diets are avoiding gluten (bread, pasta, pastries) because they think it is damaging. These people have removed grains (i.e., the "staff of life") from their diets for no other reason than they are misinformed.

LOW-CARB DIETS

Other diets, rather than limiting food to one particular item (such as grapefruit) emphasize only one class of foods. The most popular of such diets have been the low-carb diets. Carbohydrates are made up of the starches and sugars. The main source of carbohydrates for most people comes from the starch in grains. Rice contains about 90% starch, wheat is made up of about 82% starch, and corn has about 80% starch. Since carbohydrates normally provide over half of our total calories, it may seem logical to eliminate carbs to reduce weight. We are omnivores after all, so we can survive either on protein, or fat, or carbohydrates. Indeed, some peoples, such as the Inuit who live in the far north, have survived their winters for centuries by eating mostly high-fat meats and fish. But that fact does not make it a healthy diet.

Low levels of carbohydrate consumption cause the body to go into a condition called ketosis. Practitioners of low-carb diets recognize that their foods are causing this condition. In fact, one brand of low-carb diet is called the Ketogenic or "Keto" diet. According to WebMD.com,

> Ketosis is a normal metabolic process, something your body does to keep working. When it doesn't have enough carbohydrates from food for your cells to burn for energy, it burns fat instead. As part of this process, it makes ketones. If you're healthy and eating a balanced diet, your body controls how much fat it burns, and you don't normally make or use ketones. But when you cut way back on your calories or carbs, your body will switch to ketosis for energy.[8]

Mild ketosis is fine if you are limiting your total calorie intake to lose some weight. But if you are on a serious low-carb diet, and especially if you are even mildly diabetic, ketosis can increase to become a problem. Blood acidity increases, which is hard on your organs and you will have bad breath (seriously).

Basically, most fad diets try to limit the variety of foods you can eat by taking away certain foods. Thus, if you think about it, these diets reject the advice found in the Word of Wisdom and other scripture. The conclusion of such diets is that some of the foods that God and the earth have given us are actually bad for us. These new diets try to correct that mistake by rejecting those foods from our diets. Such diets come and go because they are based on faulty information. The only enduring diets have been those that recommend a sensible, healthy diet of a variety of foods.[9]

DIETARY SUPPLEMENTS

Dietary supplements are based on the same assumption that we cannot get all of our nutritional requirements from a well-balanced diet of available foods. Generally, this assumption is not true. Granted, there are many people who, due to body metabolism, disease, or age, can benefit from some form of dietary supplementation. But most people can live a very healthy life without dietary supplements.

Dietary supplements require a little explanation and a warning. For many years, the Food and Drug Administration (FDA) required that all drugs and medicines marketed in the United States show, through clinical trials, that they are both safe and effective. Pharmaceutical companies still have that requirement, so you can rest assured that your medications have had to prove their claims with statistically valid results from clinical studies on human beings. But such trials are very costly and take years to accomplish. To reduce the burden of such proof for dietary supplement companies, DSCHEA was enacted by Congress in 1994.[10] Because of this act, dietary supplements follow different rules than pharmaceuticals. Companies do have to demonstrate that their dietary supplement products are safe, but they do not have to prove they actually make you a healthier person.

A dietary supplement cannot claim to treat any disease—only clinically-proven pharmaceuticals can do that. But supplements can claim to fortify, support, strengthen, reinforce, boost, energize, supplement, sustain, and assist your normal bodily functions. If your life is busy and you feel tired from keeping up with it, such claims can sound really persuasive. "Take a pill" and you will feel energized, stronger, and happier. This message has been very successful, making dietary supplements a multibillion dollar business. Some supplement companies make their claims sound as fantastic as possible, prompting warning letters from the Food and Drug Administration (FDA) when the marketing gets too exaggerated.

A trip to your pharmacy will verify the increasing number of dietary supplements available for purchase today. First, of course, there are the general vitamins and minerals, including vitamins A, B1–B12, C, D1–D3, and vitamin E. The minerals include calcium, iron, magnesium, zinc, and potassium. Generally, a healthy diet will provide you with all the vitamins and minerals you need. To fill in any gaps in your vitamin and mineral regimen, doctors will often recommend a daily multi-vitamin pill. With vitamins and minerals, the goal is simply to prevent deficiencies. Overdosing does you no good and can, in fact, do you harm. At times, from your blood tests and discussions, your doctor may recommend that you increase your intake of a specific vitamin or mineral. This is actually what dietary supplements are meant to be. They are to supplement a gap in your nutrition that is there due to poor food choices, body metabolism, age, disease or other medical condition.

Athletes often feel the need to supplement their diet with increased levels of protein. Protein concentrates extracted from soy or dairy are available. For professional athletes, such supplementation may be needed. But again, a healthy diet should provide sufficient protein for the normal person. Protein is made up of a couple dozen different amino acids. Under the assumption that the protein in our diet does not have enough of a specific amino acid, individual amino acids such as L-lysine, lutein, and L-arginine have appeared on the market. Again, athletes and bodybuilders may deem these supplements as worthwhile. But generally, a healthy diet which includes meats, dairy, beans, and other vegetables offers a sufficient amount of protein and a broad range of amino acids.

Next come the herbal medicine dietary supplements that come from the leaves and fruit of plants not normally thought of as food. These supplements include Echinacea, saw palmetto, ginseng, ginkgo biloba, milk thistle, and St. John's wort. There have been very few clinical studies on the actual health effects these supplements claim. Several of them originated from traditional Chinese medicine and have a long tradition. Most all of these claimed benefits are anecdotal at best. Though those anecdotes have survived a long time, there is no accepted proof that such herbals are of real benefit.

Then there are the more recently developed dietary supplements to your fat intake including fish oil, flaxseed oil, and conjugated linoleic acid. Most of these supplements are designed to provide you with more poly-unsaturated fats in your diet. As noted, fish are a healthy protein source and they have a large amount of polyunsaturated fats. Thus you have an option; you can take fish oil tablets or you can simply eat more fish.

In general, a safe approach to take with dietary supplements is to start with the proposition that you can get all of the nutrients you need from your food. If you have some condition in which supplementation is needed, ask your doctor to recommend what he deems necessary. The dietary supplement industry would encourage you to take handfuls of pills, tablets, and capsules every day. But prudence, wisdom, and your doctor's guidance are needed. As stated on the FDA website regarding dietary supplements,

> Dietary supplements are intended to supplement the diets of some people, but not to replace the balance of the variety of foods important to a healthy diet. While you need enough nutrients, too much of some nutrients can cause problems. . . . Given the abundance and conflicting nature of information now available about dietary supplements, you may need help to sort the reliable information from the questionable.[11]

In conclusion, nutritionists have done a good job at getting the word out about eating a healthy diet. We can conclude that good nutritional science confirms the recommendations given in the scriptures. Lastly, the rules of a good diet change very little from day to day. The fad diets, superfoods, and latest natural remedies are distractions from that fact. We need to recognize when a proclaimed science is actually a pseudoscience and beware its claims.

NOTES

1. *The American Heritage® New Dictionary of Cultural Literacy, Third Edition.* Retrieved March 30, 2017 from Dictionary.com. http://www.dictionary.com/browse/pseudoscience.
2. Choose My Plate website, https://www.choosemyplate.gov.
3. John Forti, Strawbery Banke Museum, Portsmouth, New Hampshire, found in https://topics.blogs.nytimes.com/2009/06/05/the-manly-herb.
4. Dietary Supplement Health and Education Act of 1994: Public Law 103–417.
5. David Perlmutter, *Grain Brain* (Little, Brown and Company, 2013).
6. William Davis, *Wheat Belly*, reprint edition (Rodale Books, 2014).
7. John Yudkin & Robert H. Lustig, *Pure, White, and Deadly* (Penguin, 2013).
8. "What is Ketosis," WebMD, http://www.webmd.com/diabetes/type-1-diabetes-guide/what-is-ketosis#1
9. Andrew Weil, *Eating Well for Optimum Health* (New York: Knopf, 2000).
10. "Dietary Supplement Health and Education Act of 1994," National Institutes of Health, https://ods.od.nih.gov/About/DSHEA_Wording.aspx
11. "Tips for Dietary Supplement Users," U.S. Food & Drug Administration, https://www.fda.gov/Food/DietarySupplements/UsingDietarySupplements/ucm110567.htm

13

THE PROCESS OF LIFE

A s Latter-day Saints, we believe that this earth was created for mankind. There were specific purposes for earth life. We were meant to be born into a mortal body, learn wisdom, develop faith, and demonstrate our obedience. There would be serious challenges and dangers in this life, but those challenges were meant to be part of the learning and proving process. Earth life was a key segment of our Heavenly Father's plan. That plan was presented to us in the premortal world and we all agreed to it. We would each experience mortal life and then pass on to the next phase of our eternal life. This process is poetically described in Ecclesiastes.

> To every thing there is a season, and a time to every purpose under the heaven: A time to be born, and a time to die; a time to plant, and a time to pluck up that which is planted. (Ecclesiastes 3:1–2)

To ensure that the process of life is respected for everyone, we were given the commandment "Thou shalt not kill" (Exodus 20:13). However, the Lord fully realized that there would be men willing to kill and disrupt other's lives to gain power. Thus the Lord gave us permission to defend ourselves and our way of life.

> And again, the Lord has said that: Ye shall defend your families even unto bloodshed. Therefore for this cause were the Nephites contending with the Lamanites, to defend themselves, and their families, and their lands, their country, and their rights, and their religion. (Alma 43:47)

We believe that all men are justified in defending themselves, their friends, and property, and the government, from the unlawful assaults and encroachments of all persons in time of exigency. (D&C 134:11)

So, though it would be preferable for everyone to live peacefully through their granted years, lives are often cut short by poor decisions. Though the process of life seems like it should be a simple enough process, it is not. When considering the changes and capabilities developed by our medical sciences, the rules of defending the process of life gets even murkier and complex. Medical technologies have been developed that affect our lives both in their beginning (how we are born) and in their end (how we die). Medical researchers are not only explaining the creation of life, they are developing the power to take it into their own hands and manipulate it. By rearranging DNA, geneticists are developing abilities to remove genetic diseases, select gender, change looks, and fix health issues before a baby is even born. Many Christians, including this author, were very comfortable when only God could manipulate life to this extent. We knew we could trust God and His wisdom with the burden of making life and death decisions. We know His motives would be pure. We have less trust in mankind.

Turning now to the last chapters of life, treatments to delay death have also been developed. Medicine has developed the capability to hold us in a coma suspended between life and death for months. People go to great lengths and much expense to cheat death. You may leave directives that, at your passing, your body is to be frozen until medicine has progressed to the point of being able to restore and maintain your life again. When do such activities intrude upon the process of life? Science can give us abilities to do things that morally we should not do. We know we should defend the process of life, the concept on which the earth was formed. We must keep that fact firmly in mind as we better define our beliefs about life, death, and what power mankind should have over them.

BIOETHICS

To give science its due, the medical profession understands that it is raising very difficult moral issues. A whole new branch of philosophy called "bioethics" has been established to answer the questions that have arisen regarding the ability of science to manipulate life and death. Bioethics helps us determine the right thing to do with our new-found capabilities. Even the doctors who understand the technical aspects of new surgeries and drugs have few advantages in making philosophical decisions. The answers to these questions are often very personal, so our answers range greatly. In the text of its Roe vs. Wade ruling regarding abortion, the Supreme Court noted that,

> One's philosophy, one's experiences, one's exposure to the raw edges of human existence, one's religious training, one's attitudes toward life and family and their values, and the moral standards one establishes and seeks to observe, are all likely to influence and to color one's thinking and conclusions about abortion.[1]

Some people can be very emotional about their beliefs, even while admitting they have little technical knowledge on which to base their rage. For many, it is difficult to even discuss these issues rationally.

Bioethics is full of problems that seem to resist solutions. As part of my study on this subject, I read two books on bioethics at the same time.[2,3] One book presented the questions that bioethicists are being required to address but did not suggest any answers to them. I resented that book as it wasn't giving me insight into the answers to these hard, unsettling questions. The author of the second book gave a brief outline of those same questions and then presented his answers. I resented the second book even more because it was giving me answers with which I did not agree. These questions can overwhelm your confidence in your own sense of right and wrong. They can cause you to seriously doubt whether mankind can be trusted with the power to mold life. If you let them, these moral dilemmas can even rattle your testimony as you wonder why God has allowed mankind to unlock such secrets and to raise questions that the human race is not ready to answer.

Despite the fact that our moral compass has not been keeping up with it, medical technology continued to develop new capabilities in manipulating human life. But we should not believe that the new medical procedures being developed are evil in any way. Progress and knowledge are good; in fact, they are essential for a society to improve itself and its quality of life. It is the application of that knowledge that is challenging. How do we apply our new knowledge to benefit mankind yet stay within our ethical and moral guidelines?

The first step in this process is to educate ourselves as best we can about the issues being raised. Understanding the background and arguments of a debate allows us to look for strategies that will help people while preserving our ethics and process of life. In the next paragraphs, we will examine the moral issues that exist within medicine and perhaps take the first steps in reconciling those issues with our religious convictions.

BIRTH AND BABIES

The delivery of a baby has always been called "The Miracle of Birth." For many thousands of years of having babies, parents never really understood how a baby is conceived, developed in the womb, and born to the world. Thus, each birth was considered a miracle. But, over the centuries, the medical community has learned much about the biology of conception and birth. Most of this learning has been welcomed by society. As medical doctors and obstetricians learned more about babies and birth, more infants and their mothers were able to survive the birthing process. For example, Caesarian section delivery has been perfected over the last 50 years and has saved the lives of countless mothers and infants who would have died in a normal birthing process. Four of my own grandchildren were delivered by Caesarian delivery. No one could really argue there is an ethical problem with such a wonderful life-saving procedure.

ABORTION

But, with knowledge, came more controversial medical capabilities. The most divisive of these abilities has been that of abortion. In the early 1960s, medical research developed safer methods of aborting unwanted pregnancies. A large part of our society heralded this breakthrough as a much-needed option of birth control. But other people, often due to their religious beliefs, objected strenuously to the procedure and pressured their political leaders to make it illegal. Many loud and destructive demonstrations and protest rallies were held both in favor of and opposition to abortion. This very emotional debate continued into the 1970s and was only partially resolved when the Supreme Court ruled in 1973 in the Roe vs. Wade decision that abortion was legal. Even today there continue to be rumblings about overturning Roe vs. Wade, but the decision still stands as our law.

Much of the abortion debate has centered on its timing. When is the fetus considered to be alive? Is it alive when the heart starts beating? Is it alive when the brain has developed and the fetus responds to a stimulus? Or is the fetus alive when it can survive outside of the womb? For most Latter-day Saints, the central question may be better stated as, "At what fetal age does a person's spirit enter into its body?" The importance and logic of this question is sound. In any death, we mourn the loss of a soul, which we have defined as the combination of the spirit and the body. During earth life at least, only the soul is of importance to us. For example, at the death of an elderly grandfather, we believe his spirit leaves its body and proceeds to the next life. We grieve the loss of a beloved family member, but we don't keep the body around for very long. It is buried or cremated in just a few days. Without the spirit, the body is of no value to us. If we believe in the resurrection, we believe that body will be replaced anyway.

In regard to his spirit, we will certainly miss Grandad's presence. But we shouldn't mourn the death of his spirit, because it did not die. The spirit is eternal. In fact, in the next life we fully expect to see our grandfather's spirit again. So, if we believe that the spirit is indestructible and the body is replaceable, death should not distress us. But, in actuality the spirit and body together make up something greater than the sum of its parts. Scriptures have told us that the "worth of souls is great in the sight of the Lord" (D&C 18:10), which fits our definitions. So it is this combination of body and spirit (i.e., the soul) that we value. Death is tragic because it dissolves that combination. Until its resurrection, the spirit must wait. We don't know when that will occur. Unfortunately, we also don't know the timing of the *original* entry of the spirit into its body either. This important event has never been revealed to us and it cannot be determined by any known analytical method. So Latter-day Saints really can't answer when a fetus becomes a soul any better than the rest of the world can.

The abortion debate became so inflamed that eventually the legality of abortion was taken to the Supreme Court. Even the Supreme Court doesn't know when an embryo becomes a soul, but governments do have the power to decide the rights of those it governs. So the judicial question became, "At what age does an embryo or fetus become a person with the right to life of any other citizen?" In 1973, the Supreme Court passed down its ruling on the case of Roe vs. Wade, the court case that was used to finally determine the Court's decree on abortion. In that decision, the Court ruled that before the end of the first trimester (when the fetus is about 3 months old) a woman and her physician could decide to have an abortion, with no regulation from local, state, or federal laws. During the second trimester, when abortions become riskier, the state government can regulate the abortion procedure to ensure the mother's health is protected, but it cannot make the abortion illegal. Once the third trimester has started, state law can forbid abortions both for the well-being of the mother and to save the life of the infant. When the fetus is six months old, it is considered "viable" (or capable of living outside the uterus in the case of a premature birth or a labor-induced abortion). According to the decision by the Supreme Court, viability gives the fetus certain rights that it did not have before. Since 1973, some state governments have used the ruling's allowance to make abortions illegal after viability. Other states have made abortions legal and allow even late-term abortions.

A recent *Time* article notes that forty-four years after Roe vs. Wade, the debate about abortion in America is more divisive than ever.[4] The LDS Church has always maintained that, unless a pregnancy was caused by rape or threatens the mother's life, abortion is a serious sin. The Church will continue to be criticized for its traditional religious view on the subject. But abortion is just the first of similar questions dealing with the right to life.

IN-VITRO FERTILIZATION AND FROZEN FERTILIZED EGGS

Like Caesarian delivery, in-vitro fertilization was a very welcomed medical procedure. For decades, infertile couples had pled with their doctors to provide treatments that would help them have babies. Around 1974, the medical profession finally developed a solution in which the woman's egg could be fertilized "in-vitro" (i.e., in a test tube) and then implanted into her uterus. This technique has brought children and joy to thousands of couples. So, though a little uncomfortable with the intrusion of doctors into the conception of life, the general public welcomed this new ability. Who could argue with overjoyed parents about the benefits of this new development?

But in-vitro fertilization brought with it new moral dilemmas. If another woman's eggs are used in the implantation procedure or if a surrogate mother is used to carry the baby, to whom does the baby belong at birth? Doctors collect and then fertilize more than the number of eggs that will be implanted into the woman's uterus. They wish to be able to choose the healthiest eggs to improve the odds of a successful birth. What do we do with the extra fertilized eggs? As of 2003, nearly 400,000 embryos have been put into cold storage. About 88% of those frozen embryos were designated for future attempts at pregnancy. But many of these embryos have been stored since the late 1970s,[5] and the longer an egg is frozen, the less viable it becomes. The vast majority of these frozen embryos will never be used to create a baby, so they sit in cold storage. What do we do with these frozen embryos? Are they souls, each of which has the right to be implanted in a surrogate mother and brought to be a full-term baby? Or are they simply frozen bits of tissue that are being stored for no reason?

IS A FERTILIZED EGG A SOUL?
A PERSONAL OPINION

Is a fertilized egg a soul? Does a spirit child of our Heavenly Father enter into a baby at the earliest stage of its development or later? I am hesitant to state my own answer to this question, but I am going to do so because I think my epiphany on the subject is a good example of how we can blend scientific findings with our religious beliefs to make better sense of the world.

Over my life, I have tried to stay current on the developments in genetics and human reproduction. The issue of what to do with frozen fertilized eggs was just one of the many questions that I put on a mental shelf. Over those years, I simply didn't have the information to answer such questions. But in the course of my reading, I discovered one fact that changed my outlook and belief as to whether a newly fertilized egg is a soul. That fact allowed me to take this one question off my mental shelf and develop an opinion that made sense to me and is now part of my belief system.

That fact was this: when a woman goes through a normal conception, the fertilized egg within her needs to make its way to her uterus and implant itself there. For a successful implantation, the woman's hormones have to be correctly balanced so her uterus is primed and ready for the implantation. The fertilized egg must settle in and the uterus must then establish vascular contact so it can provide blood, nourishment, and waste removal to the developing embryo. This is a very complicated process and, if the woman's body chemistry is not right, the egg will not implant. In fact, it is estimated that *over half* of fertilized eggs do not successfully implant in the uterus and are consequently flushed out of the woman's body.[6] This is a significant level of failure. In fact, it is so high that the American College of Obstetricians and Gynecologists does not consider a woman pregnant until her fertilized egg has successfully implanted itself in her uterus.

The implications of this finding are significant. If a spirit enters the cell of an egg upon its fertilization, as many people profess, then over half of our Heavenly Father's spirit children die before they are a week old. Their "bodies," made up of only a few cells, will never have a mind, nerves, physical sensations, or self-awareness. By this definition, over half of our spiritual brothers and sisters will never see, hear, or feel. Though we certainly don't know exactly what constitutes an earth life, it is hard to believe that only being a few cells counts as our mortal journey. The earth was created so that we could have a body, develop faith, and learn obedience. Yes, the world is a dangerous place. But it makes no sense that our Creator engineered the birthing process such that half of His spirit children never get past the first step of their journey. So, in this author's opinion, a fertilized egg is not yet a soul. Whether you agree with that conclusion or not, this is an example of combining what we learn from gospel study with medical findings and logic to come to a resolution of such an issue. Patience, study, and thought appear to be the only way we can develop understanding and a response to some of today's bioethical challenges.

CLONING

Cloning of animals is the scientific method of taking the egg of a female and reproducing it. The resulting baby animal will essentially have no father. This technically challenging procedure involves removing the nucleus of a newly-fertilized embryotic cell that is ready to grow into a fetus and replacing it with the nucleus of a cell from a mature animal. The embryotic cell is poised and ready to start creating a baby animal. Through biochemical prompts, the embryonic cell signals the adult DNA in the transplanted nucleus to start making copies of itself so that new cells can be made. The adult DNA remembers the process of DNA separation and embryonic growth. The nucleus cooperates and begins DNA replication so new cells can be made to grow the embryo. After a few days in a petri dish, the embryo is placed into the uterus of a surrogate mother. There it continues to grow, develops into a baby, and is delivered into the world like any other newborn. The public had been aware of the concept of cloning for decades. But it was not until 1997 when a sheep named Dolly was actually cloned in Scotland that the public needed to confront the reality. Dolly was a clone because she had the exact genetic make-up of her mother—or her sister depending on how you define the relationship. No male DNA at all was involved in Dolly's creation. Since there are billions of cells in your body, conceivably you could be the source of billions of clones. It is a strange concept to consider. Not surprisingly, science fiction television shows and movies quickly moved to examine the possibilities of the new technology with shows like *Gattaca* (1997), *Andromeda* (2000), *Star Wars: Attack of the Clones* (2002), and numerous others.

Despite the hype, cloning is not that scary. An identical twin is a clone of its sibling, and twins are simply not that threatening. But cloning will probably never find a significant place for itself in our future. It is an extremely expensive and inefficient system of reproduction. In the present process, cloning is too complex to be used routinely in livestock production. Cloning humans makes even less sense. Our earth certainly does not need any help in the area of reproduction, as our rising populations will attest. The natural approach to reproduction, by combining DNA instead of simply copying it, gives the human population its diversity and breadth. Several international accords prohibit the cloning of humans and there is little economic impetus to break those laws. This is one bioethical issue that will probably pass from public debate due to simple impracticality.

THE STEM CELL DEBATE

After an egg is fertilized, it begins to cleave. It becomes two cells, which become four, which become eight, and so on. Between four and six days, the developing embryo is called a blastocyst. The blastocyst is a round ball of cells, with an outer layer and a few dozen internal cells. These internal cells are called the inner cell mass and they are very special cells indeed. It is important to note that the blastocyst is still a pre-implantation embryo as it has not yet attached itself to the uterus.

The inner cell mass cells are also called embryonic stem cells. Stem cells are special because they can become any cell that the body needs to build itself. As the embryo develops, the stem cells continue to divide. Gradually the stem cells proceed down different paths as their DNA commands. At about two weeks old, the embryonic stem cells differentiate. If they become ectodermal cells, they are on the path to become the spinal cord, brain, nerves, and skin. If they become mesodermal cells, they will eventually become blood cells, a heart, muscle, or bone. Lastly, inner cell mass stem cells can become endodermal, meaning they will develop into the gut, liver, lungs, pancreas, bladder, etc. Over the next couple of months of embryonic development, the ectodermal, mesodermal, and endodermal cells will differentiate even further. For example, some of the fetus' ectodermal cells differentiate to become neural stem cells. As such, neural stem cells can only become nerves. They have lost their earlier potential to become skin cells or any other kind of cell for that matter. At this point, the stem cells in the fetus have differentiated to the point that they are no longer embryonic. They have become adult stem cells. Neural stem cells will continue to create nerve cells for the baby throughout its childhood and adult life. This differentiation is obviously an important transformation that needs to take place in the embryo's development. Embryonic stem cells must lose their flexibility or potency to become any cell in the body. They need to specialize in the tasks for which they have been programmed.[7]

By 1998, the technology had been developed to not only remove the inner stem cells of the blastocyst but to maintain them and to cause them to grow and divide in a petri dish. Considering the blastocyst is barely large enough to see with the naked eye, the removal of living cells from its middle is impressive enough. But the larger challenge was to promote the stem cells to continue to multiply without differentiating themselves into ectodermal, mesodermal, and endodermal cells. With care and direction, it was deemed possible to grow new organs for implantation. A failing kidney, liver, or heart could be replaced without the need for a donor.

Advances in cloning and stem cell research shared science news headlines in the late 1990s. Then a few people proposed a "what if" line of research. What if a rich man wanted to clone, say, a replacement organ, limb, or a whole new body? Science had already learned from its cloning experiments that biologists could remove the nucleus of just one cell from our rich man and place it into an evacuated embryonic stem cell. We knew that we could maintain the stem cells on culture plates indefinitely and researchers were in the process of learning how to direct the specialization of those stem cells. Theoretically, the rich man could have a reservoir of stem cells with his DNA in them made up that could then be used to grow replacement organs, skin grafts, bone marrow, or anything else he would need to extend his life. Since all these cells and organs would have his own DNA in them, the rich man would not have to worry about his body rejecting a new implant. Regarding this hypothesis, Dr. Christopher Scott, past Director of the Stanford Program on Stem Cells in Society noted,

> In essence, an early human embryo would need to be made—then destroyed—to obtain the cells inside. Of course, once the moral and medical implications of such an experiment became clear, all hell broke loose.[7]

Alarmists warned of a society in which the rich would pay women to donate eggs to be sent to a lab to grow organs, limbs, and entire bodies for their use. The images bordered on the macabre. Though the technology was still in its hypothetical stage, the public and our elected officials reacted emotionally to the possibility. In August 2001, President George Bush, in a nationally televised broadcast, announced that he was restricting federal funding of stem cell research such that no funds could be used to generate any new stem cell lines. In 2005, in his State of the Union address, President Bush promised "to ensure that human embryos are not created for experimentation or grown for body parts, and that human life is never bought and sold as a commodity." To their credit, I doubt if any of the leading stem cell researchers had plans to open up a storefront to buy embryos and sell body parts. In actuality, scientists have always managed to regulate themselves. The National Academy of Science published "Guidelines for Human Embryonic Stem Cell Research" in 2005 to establish rules for growing and handling blastocysts, obtaining full consent from donors, and preventing human cloning. The guideline also prevents allowing a blastocyst to develop for longer than 14 days. (At 15 days, the blastocyst starts to develop into an embryonic disk, the first stage of embryo formation. By definition of the word, embryos are never used for stem cell research.)

So, should you care if stem cell research continues? That would probably depend on your opinion of the worth of this line of medical research. Stem cells can replace dying cells in a person's body. Consider for a moment the power they could have in relieving pain and suffering in the world and improving the quality of life of millions. Parkinson's disease is a chronic and progressive movement disorder caused by the impairment or death of neurons in the brain. It afflicts nearly one million people in the U.S.A.[8] Research is being done to determine if stem cells can generate neurons to reverse this effect. Similar research is occurring to see if stem cells can treat Alzheimer's disease, diabetes, heart disease, and other medical conditions that require new cells to replace non-functional cells in our organs. Thus, we have a moral dilemma. Presently, embryonic stem cells can only be harvested from human blastocysts, but the potential for resolving dementia, the effects of aging, and human disease is significant. It is a difficult, morally complex issue.

DEATH AND DYING

Just as medical advances have affected our conception and birthing process, they have affected our dying process. Throughout most of our history, men have not been able to decide when they died. When their time was up, they passed away. But, as has been mentioned, times have changed and we now have choices we never had before. Naturally we would all want the option to live a long, healthy life and then die peacefully while asleep in our bed at home. But our choices are usually somewhat more difficult than that.

We are all aware of the commandment "Thou shalt not kill." Murder cuts off the process of life and the earthly experiences that the victim should have had. Once taken, a life cannot be replaced. Since there can be no restitution, a full repentance of the act is not possible (D&C 42:14). As mentioned earlier, there are exceptions to this punishment, such as killing someone in a war or in self-defense. But moral dilemmas still exist around this commandment, such as whether the death penalty for convicted felons should exist.

Suicide also prematurely ends a mortal life. Years ago, Church leaders taught that suicide was akin to murder, with severe consequences in the next life. But since then, the Church has softened its stance on the subject.[9] Each one of us has a strong self-preservation feature built into our being. If we are drowning, we will struggle, even unconsciously, to reach the water's surface to breathe and live on. Those who commit suicide due to depression reject that basic instinct to live and, it has been realized, cannot be in their right minds if they accomplish it. It has been an interesting evolution of doctrine that should give us hope that moral issues can be better understood over time.

THE END OF LIFE DECISION

We can recognize the progression of the process of life in the infirmities of old age. We are born helpless, but we grow and mature. Most of us enjoy the bloom of health and fitness during the third and fourth decades of life. But in the succeeding decades, our bodies start to break down. Our pains and infirmities are confirmation that the process of life includes our passing. Obviously, as we pass through our middle age years and enter our elderly years, we are going to use medical and pharmaceutical advances to extend our lives and improve their quality. Any person over the age of 50 is probably taking at least one prescription medicine.

We have much to live for in those years. But those pharmaceutical treatments and medical procedures have continued to push our life spans well into our eighties and nineties. This may sound wonderful at first. But as an elderly father is first confined to a wheel chair, then becomes bedridden, then falls into senility and dementia, the joy starts to abate. At first, it is obvious that we should take all medical steps possible to keep our elderly loved ones alive for as long as possible. But when is doing so interrupting the process of life? Long term comas are truly a suspension between life and death, so how long should we keep a loved one there? As quality of life diminishes, the heart-wrenching question that may need to be answered is, "Should the life-extending technology and medications be turned off?" The ethical question that bothers many elderly is, "Is it suicide if I do?"

When my family and I first moved to Flagstaff, Arizona, an elderly man in our ward, Clyde, became our friend and home teacher. Clyde's legs were so unsteady that I worried that he would not make it up our front stairs when he came to visit. Within the year, Clyde's health declined to the point he could no longer attend church or visit our home. Clyde was in constant pain for a long time. His kidneys were failing and he was undergoing painful dialysis. Finally, Clyde decided to discontinue all medications and medical treatments. My son asked me if Clyde's decision was not the same as suicide. I had no idea how to answer him. Dimly, I felt that choosing to discontinue the medications that caused a pain-filled life was not the same as suicide. But it was an issue I had left on my mental shelf of unanswered questions for many years. Now that I am approaching the end of my own life, I am forced to reconsider the issue and make my own decisions.

When you consult your scriptures, you will see that there is no commandment to take your pills and to allow surgeries that may or may not extend your life. As I approach the end of my own life, I realize there will be a point where I will stop fighting the fate of old age. Though such a decision may lead to an earlier end to my life, the remaining time I do have on the earth will be a better quality without the drugs and recoveries from surgery. Every case is different, and you have the right and obligation to make your own decisions. When does the cost to a person's health, dignity, and happiness outweigh the benefit of staying alive?

There are trade-offs. Certainly, with enough medication, any pain can be dulled at the expense of a clear mind and mental acuity. After much internal debate on this issue, I have personally concluded that it is not wrong to end medical treatment being administered by concerned doctors who want the best for you. No elderly person should be burdened with the guilt of thinking they are committing suicide by halting painful surgeries, long-term dialysis, and drugs that hamper mental acuity.

ADVANCE MEDICAL DIRECTIVE

With the ability of our medical technology to keep an elderly person alive for years has come a lot of very sad stories about drawn-out deaths of elderly people who certainly did not deserve them. Their families mistakenly believed that their loved ones would recover and return to their normal lives, despite the counsel of their doctors. A number of books have been published by medical professionals who are tired of seeing such needless pain and suffering of the elderly.[10,11,12] Doctors are generally wonderful counselors, who are committed to educating the patient and their family about their options. In the modern Hippocratic Oath, doctors pledge, "I will apply, for the benefit of the sick, all measures which are required . . ." so they will do everything they can for their patients. But the oath continues and doctors also promise to avoid overtreatment, so they must decide when further treatments will be of limited or no use.[13] In regard to the care of your beloved grandfather, there are good reasons you should listen to his doctors. Medical professionals have seen cases similar to your grandfather's, and they know how those turned out. They have the technical knowledge to comprehend what is occurring to your grandfather's biological mechanisms. They almost certainly have wrestled with many such treatment decisions in the past. Because of their concern, doctors also want to factor your grandfather's desires into their recommendations.

Thus there is an ongoing campaign to get people to prepare and sign an "advance medical directive" or living will. Through this document, you can let your family, doctors, the hospital, and our legal system know your desires for your end-of-life care. You can let it be known if you ever want to be attached to an inhaler or a feeding tube. You can declare if you want to be resuscitated if your heart stops. You can indicate when you would like to be transferred to hospice care. You can describe the circumstances under which you want the machines that are keeping you alive to be turned off or under which you want medications to be discontinued. Since you can't know exactly when or how you will decline, these directives ask for details of your wishes. While still in your right mind and before anyone can object, you can make your desires clear to your family and your doctors. There are multiple websites available that provide templates for you to write out your wishes and medical directives.

Besides the living will, you should also sit your children down with you and explain to them, in no uncertain terms, your desires. This does two things. First, it should spare your children the guilt of discontinuing the machines or medications that are keeping you alive. It was your decision, not theirs. Secondly, it helps prevent your children from making decisions that contradict your desires (since, after you have lost your mental faculties, your children or designated agent can easily do just that). For these reasons, I have tried to ensure that my own children fully understand my intentions and desires. Since we believe in eternal families in the life hereafter, my children now know that their dad will be furious with them if they do not follow these particular instructions to the letter.

Lastly, everyone should be aware of the option of hospice care. Hospice is a type of care very different than what you will find elsewhere. In hospitals or nursing homes, the goal is to prolong your life. In hospice care, the goal is to make the last days of your life as comfortable and pleasant as possible. It is a completely different mindset and approach, which can be disturbing to those who are not ready for it, but very comforting for those who are.

NOTES

1. "Roe v. Wade," FindLaw, https://caselaw.findlaw.com/us-supreme-court/410/113.html.
2. Thomas Shannon & Nicholas Kockler, *An Introduction to Bioethics* (Mahwah, NJ: Paulist Press, 2009).
3. Gilbert Meilaender, *Bioethics* (Grand Rapids, MI: William B. Eerdmans, 2005).
4. Mary Eberstadt,"*How the Abortion Debate Rocked Progressivism,*" *Time*, Feb 6 2017, 32.
5. "How Many Frozen Human Embryos Are Available for Research?" RAND Corp. Study, (2003) by D.I. Hoffman, GL Zellman, CC Fair, JF Mayer, JG Zeitz, WE Gibbons, and TG Turner.
6. "Which Fertilized Eggs Will Become Healthy Human Fetuses?" Stanford University Medical Center, Science Daily 4 October 2010 and "Physiology of Implantation," T.G. Kennedy, 10th World Congress on In-vitro Fertilization and Assisted Reproduction, Vancouver Canada, May 1997
7. Christopher Thomas Scott, *Stem Cell Now* (London: Penguin, 2006).
8. Parkinson's Disease Foundation, www.pdf.org.
9. M. Russell Ballard, "Suicide: Some Things We Know and Some We Do Not," *Ensign*, Oct. 1987.
10. Atul Gawande, *Being Mortal* (New York: Metropolitan Books, 2014), 9, 30–31.
11. Angelo E. Volandes, *The Conversation* (New York: Bloomsbury Publishing, 2015), 78.
12. Haider Warraich, *Modern Death* (New York: St. Martin's Press, 2017).
13. John Hopkins, Sheridan Libraries, Bioethics, Modern Hippocratic Oath, http://guides.library.jhu.edu/c.php?g=202502&p=1335759.

14

SCIENCE AND RELIGION EPILOGUE

n 2012, the European Organization for Nuclear Research (CERN) announced that their physicists had finally proven the existence of the Higgs boson, a particle of matter predicted to exist by equations in particle physics. The announcement, like previous such discoveries, was taken by some as yet another finding that reduces the need for or existence of God.[1] This tiresome logic declares that as humanity determines how the universe was created, the argument for the existence of God is somehow weakened. But the answers to the questions of how the Creation occurred have never been hidden. Mankind was meant to discover the mechanisms of the universe and learn how to use them for our benefit.

To argue effectively that God does not exist, critics need to answer the question of *who* built the universe, not *how* it was done. Determining what tools and materials were used to build a house tells you nothing about the builder. Who directed the Creation? There are only two possible answers. Either God (by whatever name you wish to call Him) or random chance accomplished this miracle. The universe either has a Creator or it does not. The main argument against chance and good luck creating the Universe is that random, undirected events cannot create organized, complex, and beautiful creations. What is the probability that random chance could have created the universe, Earth, and life? One in trillions. There are billions of suns and planets in the universe, but that does not change the slim odds of life developing on our world. New findings in science should never shake a testimony, as long as you know the correct questions to ask and have a good foundation of understanding.

On the other hand, scientific findings have presented facts that may require changes to our perceptions of life and the gospel. How should we interpret the account of Noah's ark? Who wrote the scriptures? Do the findings of genetic decoding change our perceptions of the biological history of the earth? The answers to these questions are more complex than anyone would have thought possible in past centuries. The fact that mankind can now manipulate the medical processes of birth, life, and death creates new responsibilities for mankind. Each bioethical issue must be judged with a conviction to preserve the process of life for Heavenly Father's children so each can accomplish the goals of earth life. Today we have more information at our fingertips than ever before in history. With new facts come new understandings. We should neither fear nor reject new paradigms. They guide us to a better grasp of truth.

Many people believe in God and still believe the findings of science, adjusting their understanding of the gospel to new discoveries. This is sometimes difficult. But if we start our investigation with the premise that God lives and evidence defines truth, we can figure it out. Such efforts will be rewarded as our understanding of the earth, the universe, the purpose of life, and the gospel all come together to support one another. There is a comfort in knowing that your belief system cannot be threatened by the latest findings in science. That comfort is a result of a strong mental testimony. But a mental testimony takes work. Reading good books and keeping up with new developments in science is a task in itself. Meditating on how these new ideas bolster your perceptions, or require you to change them, is also needed. But the result is confidence that your beliefs are supported by evidence. That mental confidence will bolster your spiritual testimony.

The Savior taught us to recognize teachers of truth when He declared that "every good tree bringeth forth good fruit" (Matt 7:17). Science has brought forth too much good fruit to doubt it is a good tree. When we better understand our physical world, we better understand the gospel as well. Through this continuing process, we can come to know that,

> If thou shalt ask, thou shalt receive revelation upon revelation, knowledge upon knowledge, that thou mayest know the mysteries and peaceable things—that which bringeth joy, that which bringeth life eternal. (D&C 42:61)

Sometimes we will receive those revelations through prayer. Other times we will receive it by reading a science book. But from both sources we can come to know the mysteries and peaceable things that bring joy and life eternal.

NOTE

1. Lawrence M. Krauss, *A Universe from Nothing* (New York: Simon & Schuster, 2012), xvii.

ABOUT THE AUTHOR

Scott R. Frazer (PhD Chemistry, University of Arizona) joined The Church of Jesus Christ of Latter-day Saints when he was nineteen years old and left on a Church mission to Mexico City a year later. Upon his return to Colorado, he finished up his bachelor's degree in chemistry, married his wife, Cheri, and then completed his doctorate in analytical chemistry. His work history includes research roles in a variety of industries. Since joining the Church, Scott has studied the overlap between his religious beliefs and the sciences. In the course of discussions with many LDS friends, Scott discovered that there is a large gap between science and religion that many Church members simply do not know how to fill. Scott's writings are dedicated to simplifying this process. Having lived in numerous locations across the US, Scott and Cheri now reside in Saratoga Springs, Utah, to be nearer their four children and their families.

Scan to visit

www.scottrfrazer.com